UNIVERSITY OF BRISTOL
Food Refrigeration and
Process Engineering Research Centre
F R P E R C Churchill Building
Langford, Bristol. BS18 7DY
Tel: + 44 (0)117 928 9239   Fax: + 44 (0)117 928 9314

Food Processing

Food Processing

Edited by Richard Cottrell

Proceedings of the Ninth
British Nutrition Foundation Annual Conference

The Parthenon Publishing Group
International Publishers in Science, Technology & Education

Casterton Hall, Carnforth,
Lancs, LA6 2LA, U.K.

120 Mill Road, Park Ridge,
New Jersey, U.S.A.

Published in the UK and Europe by
The Parthenon Publishing Group Limited,
Casterton Hall, Carnforth,
Lancs. LA6 2LA, England.

Published in the USA by
The Parthenon Publishing Group Inc.,
120 Mill Road,
Park Ridge,
New Jersey 07656

ISBN 1 85070 256 X

First published 1989

Typeset by H & H Graphics, Blackburn

Printed in Great Britain by
Antony Rowe Ltd, Chippenham, Wiltshire

Contents

Acknowledgements

The British Nutrition Foundation wishes to express its appreciation to all those who agreed to speak at the Conference and to provide papers for publication, to Fari Kamalati and Suzanne Barritt for their help in the preparation of the typescript and to Parthenon Publishing Group for their co-operation in the publishing of this book.

List of contributors

A. J. Bailey
Director,
AFRC Food Research Institute,
Langford,
Bristol BS18 7DY

A. E. Bender
2 Willow Vale,
Fetcham,
Leatherhead,
Surrey KT22 9TE

P. G. Boseley
Director of Research and Development,
Agricultural Genetics Company,
Unit 154/155 Cambridge Science Park,
Milton Road,
Cambridge CB4 4GG

J. J. Connell
Former Director,
Torry Reseach Station,
61 Burnieboozle Crescent,
Aberdeen AB1 8NR

R. M. Faulks
AFRC Institute of Food Research
Colney Lane,
Norwich,
Norfolk NR4 7UA

D. L. Georgala
Directo,
Agricultural and Food Research
    Council,
AFRC Institute of Food Research,
Reading Laboratory,
Shinfield,
Reading RG2 9AT

F. Harding
Technical Director,
Milk Marketing Board,
Thames Ditton,
Surrey KT7 0EL

J. Hawthorn
Emeritus Professor of Food Science,
University of Strathclyde,
3 Greenwood Drive,
Bearsden,
Glasgow,
Strathclyde C61 2NA

J. C. Hughes
Head of Potato Processing Group,
AFRC Food Research Institute,
Colney Lane,
Norwich,
Norfolk NR4 7UA

R. W. Hunt
Industrial Food Product
    Development Manager,
Procter & Gamble Limited,
Whitley Road,
Longbenton,
PO Box Forest Hall, No 21,
Newcastle-upon-Tyne NE12 9TS

R. C. Righelato
Director of Research and Development,
Tate & Lyle plc,
The University,
PO Box 68, Whiteknights,
Reading, Berkshire RG6 2BX

J. Selman
Deputy Head of Experimental
    Processing and Packaging,
Campden Food Preservation R A,
Chipping Campden,
Glos GL55 6DL

B. Spencer
Director of Research and Development,
Flour Milling and Baking R A,
Chorleywood,
Herts WD3 5SN

E. Widdowson
Department of Medicine,
Addenbrooke's Hospital,
Level 5,
Hills Road,
Cambridge CB2 2QQ

Preface

The ever increasing pace of advances in methods of production and processing of foods, and the impact of economic pressures on the choices made by the farmer, the food manufacturer and the retailer of food, have led to revolutionary changes in the products available to the consumer. These changes may have appreciable impact on the nutrition, and consequently the health, of the people of this country. It it one of the functions of the British Nutrition Foundation to encourage scientists, including food technologists, to assess the effects of development, many of which may be inspired by considerations other than nutrition.

The conference on which this book is based was designed to allow specialists in the technology of food processing to discuss, with specialists in other disciplines, those aspects of the changes occurring in the food chain that might have nutritional importance, and to allow those attending to understand something of the reasoning behind the choices of feedstock production methods, processing technology, packaging materials, transportation environments and display techniques used in the modern retail food industry. A subsidiary aim was to encourage greater attention to the nutritional consequences of these choices by those who make major decisions in the industry.

The activities of the food industry, often driven by forces beyond the industry's control, have a fundamental impact on the foods available to the consumer and the purchasing decisions of the shopper. Distortions can arise in the nutrient intake of individuals, both because of unforeseen consequences of the introduction of new technologies (Professor Bender mentions some examples in his contribution to this book), and because of ignorance or misinformation. The Foundation aims to encourage public knowledge of nutrition and to foster more attention to nutritional exellence in developments of new products and processing.

This book is intended to provide an overview of this complex and rapidly developing field so that the interested reader can begin to understand the complex web of factors that determine the direction of new developments in the food industry and the probable nutritional consequences of the changes taking place.

E. Widdowson

Department of Medicine
Addenbrooke's Hospital
Level 5
Hills Road
Cambridge CB2 2QQ

June 1987

Foreword

Agriculture has developed continuously since its inception in pre-history, and food processing has advanced a trifle since the earliest recorded examples in Ancient Egypt. But at no time in history has the rate of change been so breathtaking. Improvements in cereal and vegetable crops allow greater yields and disease and pest resistance, better handling and storage tolerance, and greater variety. Developments in animal breeding, husbandry and butchery techniques allow greater efficiency, improved microbiological and nutritional characteristics and better organoleptic quality in the meat offered to the consumer. Food processing allows an enormous variety of products to be presented at the supermarkets in a safe, palatable and attractive form, often at remarkably low cost. Modern cooking methods, coupled with appropriate transport and storage technology, mean that meal preparation times in the home can be a fraction of those of a few years ago with no sacrifice in quality.

Compared to the enormous attention given to the technical and economic details of each of these advances relatively little is known of the nutritional effects that may result. In the development of vegetable crops nutritional value is rarely considered and choices are sometimes made that are nutritionally or even toxicologically exceptionable. The popular Golden Delicious apple provides an example in the nutritional area, since it is much lower in vitamin C than many traditional varieties, and, of the toxicological issues, one is that potato varieties are available that are lower in solanins than many commercially popular types. Considerable cereal breeding programmes have been undertaken with scant regard for the nutritional content of the food that will be made from the crop and oilseed rape has been specifically developed to *reduce* the level of an essential fatty acid in the oil.

Nor is the food processing industry blameless. Very little attention has

13

been given, for example, to nutritional matters in the development of such fundamentally important processes as microwave or extrusion cooking. Nutrition, in relation to food technology, may seem of little importance in our highly developed society where the only conspicuous and common nutrition-related disease is obesity. On the other hand in the third world, food preservation offers a major benefit to many impoverished and undernourished peoples. Technological development needs to take account of the nutritional consequences of what is done to a food in the food processing factory, and plant and animal breeding programmes must not sacrifice nutritional quality for mere quantity.

J. Hawthorn

University of Strathclyde
3 Greenwood Drive
Bearsden
Glasgow
Strathclyde C61 2NA

1
Modern food processing

D. L. GEORGALA

INTRODUCTION

The availability of a reliable food supply is vital to each of us. Food policy issues loom large in national and international politics, and the production and processing of food is a major economic activity in the modern world. Major media attention has been focused on food and health questions. The technical basis underlying our food supply must therefore be of considerable interest.

This review examines the size and scope of the UK food industry. It also discusses the changes taking place in consumer needs, and in the pattern of the national diet. The development of key areas of processing and preservation will be outlined together with the role these play in providing today's food shopping basket in response to changing market needs. It also includes some specific comments on the question of additives. The paper concludes with some observations on likely future developments, although speculations of this type are fraught with uncertainty.

Consumer expenditure on retail food and non-alcoholic beverages in the UK is currently running at around £28 000 million a year. About 80% of this is for processed and packaged food and beverages, and the remaining 20% is spent on unpacked agricultural and horticultural commodities. We spend an additional £9 000 million on food purchased in catering/fast food outlets and £14 000 million a year in all on alcoholic drinks. The expenditure on food and non-alcoholic beverages now represents about 15% of total consumer expenditure – and has been dropping, although volume of food eaten has been maintained or increased. The food industry accounts for about 9% of total capital spending in the UK manufacturing industry, and has a workforce of about 450 000.

The broad distribution of expenditure on different commodities (Table 1) has changed relatively slowly over time. Within this pattern, there are some 50 000 different food and drink products available in Britain, and the average family buys about 300 different types of food product in a year. Despite the general stability in our diet, it is worth remembering that in recent years there have been some quite notable trends in purchasing patterns. Whole milk, beef, bacon, sugar, butter have gone down for example, while demand has increased for skimmed milk, poultry, soft margarines, wholemeal bread, fruit juices etc.

Over the years, the UK has become increasingly self-sufficient in food and drinks. The picture is very complicated because we import some foods which we could produce here, e.g. some meat products, cheese and drinks. Overall we are about 60% self-sufficient, and about 75% self-sufficient in those foods which we could reasonably be expected to produce here. We also export considerable quantities of food and drink. About 7% of all food and drink products manufactured in the UK are

Table 1.1   UK domestic food expenditure

Food product	%
Meat, poultry, bacon	27
Breads, cereals	20
Dairy products	13
Vegetables	12
Fruit	6
Sugar, preserves, confectionery	5
Beverages	4
Oils and fats	4
Fish	4
Eggs	2
Miscellaneous	3

exported. We are the world's seventh largest exporter of food and agricultural products.

For the purpose of this review processing may be defined as the application of culinary and industrial arts to the preparation of foods. From some press coverage, you might sometimes think that this is an invention of our own times. This is far from so. A food processing industry of some sort has existed since the dawn of history, and the development of this industry has been closely intertwined with social developments, and is responsive to the needs and demands of consumers. Many traditional foods and beverages, for example, butter, flour, bread, tea, beer, are examples of processed foods, and could not exist without some form of processing.

Most forms of processing – cleaning, cutting, mixing, adding flavours, cooking, boiling, baking – have been known and used in kitchens for centuries. Many of these techniques have been adapted and scaled-up to form the basis of today's food industry.

There are very good reasons behind this long history, and it should be particularly emphasised that processing technology has been and still is used for three main purposes:

(1) To convert agricultural produce and fish to palatable attractive foods.
(2) To ensure the preservation and safety of food products for availability out of season.
(3) To ensure the safer distribution of foods to urban populations distant from agricultural production.

It is sometimes forgotten that much agricultural produce needs considerable work and modification to make it palatable. For example, cereals are virtually inedible without milling and conversion into porridge, bread or fermented drinks. Other foods, such as cassava, are quite toxic in their native states and require appropriate elution by water or cooking before they can be eaten safely. By and large most people, over the ages, have preferred to eat meat which has been cooked in one way or another, rather than tackle raw flesh. The same could be said of fish.

Turning to preservation, many agricultural products are generated on a seasonal basis, and from the dawn of history methods for preserving foods have been applied by both nomadic populations and settled civilisations. Some Roman food products and processes would be quite recognisable today!

What has happened of course, is that, with the Industrial Revolution bringing greater urbanisation and specialisation of lifestyles, traditional processing and distribution of foods has been extended and developed into a larger economic activity. Some 80% of our population is in urban communities at densities of over a thousand persons per square kilometre, and it is simply not practical for each of us to grow our own food.

Within this modern society there are further fundamental changes taking place. These have, and will continue to have, a great effect on the types of food products demanded by the consumer (Table 2). Convenience has become an essential requirement in many of today's food products, and some of the reasons are not hard to find, for example in the changing pattern of meals and the changing lifestyle of women. The increase in single person households is another factor. A further major development has been the enormous growth of the supermarket industry with its impact on shopping patterns and the retailing of food products.

Table 1.2   Meal patterns and preparations

Eating occasions (1982)

48%	of all respondents had only 1 meal per day
72%	had 4 or more snacks per day

Working wives (1984)

20.3%	of wives worked full time
20.4%	of wives work part time
40.7%	total of working wives

Main meal preparation (1982)

On weekdays, 55% spent 30 minutes or less

(From Mintel, April 1986)

Food legislation

It should also be noted that over the past century, legislation has been developed to ensure the quality and safety of the food supply. The work of early food chemists in the 19th century, men such as Frederick Accum and John Mitchell, led to wide public and parliamentary concern about the massive adulteration of foods (Figure 1). Accum showed that almost all foods were adulterated. Well recognised examples were alum, used to extend flour in bread, the use of sulphuric acid to accelerate the ageing of beer, and the addition of dried hedgerow leaves to tea.

The first real food legislation came in the 1860s and 1870s, setting up the principles of control, and the appointment of public analysts and powers of enforcement. Further major legislative steps were taken in 1928, and again in 1955, giving Ministers very wide powers to regulate foods.

Today, the 1984 Food Act embodies the key aspects of food legislation, and there is now a very wide range of regulations covering the handling, processing and sale of foods. Primarily these are to ensure wholesomeness and safety of foods, and to ensure that food is sold in a way which does not deceive (Figure 2).

FOOD PROCESSING AND PRESERVATION

A few examples of food processing serve to illustrate the role and history of food processing and preservation.

Butter was produced in India at least 4000 years ago and it has been known as a product in Europe for several hundred years at least. Traditionally made by hand, at the site of milk production, the development of an effective cream separator in 1878 paved the way for centralised production in the large creameries we have today.

This industrial development has had additional social benefits, in that centralised dairies could apply new technologies, such as pasteurisation, and improved hygiene to eliminate the disease problems which were associated with milk in past times, including tuberculosis and typhoid. Table 3 shows figures which give a stark reminder of the benefits we have derived from the pasteurisation and hygienic processing of milk and milk products by the dairy industry.

A

TREATISE

ON

ADULTERATIONS OF FOOD,

AND CULINARY POISONS.

EXHIBITING

The Fraudulent Sophistications of

BREAD, BEER, WINE, SPIRITOUS LIQUORS,
TEA, COFFEE, CREAM, CONFECTIONERY,
VINEGAR, MUSTARD, PEPPER, CHEESE,
OLIVE OIL, PICKLES,
AND OTHER ARTICLES EMPLOYED IN DOMESTIC ECONOMY.

AND

METHODS OF DETECTING THEM.

———

By Fredrick Accum,

OPERATIVE CHEMIST, AND MEMBER OF THE PRINCIPAL
ACADEMIES AND SOCIETIES OF ARTS AND SCIENCES
IN EUROPE.

———

Philadelphia:

PRINTED AND PUBLISHED BY AB'M SMALL

1820.

Figure 1.1

043414

Food Act 1984

CHAPTER 30

A Table showing the derivation of the provisions of this consolidation Act will be found at the end of the Act. The Table has no official status.

ARRANGEMENT OF SECTIONS

PART I

FOOD GENERALLY

A

Figure 1.2

Table 1.3   Outbreaks of disease due to milk and milk products (UK)

Disease	Number of cases		
	1912-37	1938-60	1961-70
Streptococcal infections	5331	875	0
Diptheria	773	37	0
Enteric fever (i.e. typhoid and paratyphoid fevers)	3229	334	0

(From Topley and Wilson 1975, Edward Arnold, London.)

Even a relatively modern product, such as margarine, has a long history. Margarine was invented by a Frenchman, Mege-Mourie, in the 1860s, to win a government prize for an effective, cheaper substitute for butter. The original product would not sell in today's supermarkets, but 100 years of research and development has ensured that there are a wide range of margarine-type products now meeting different consumer requirements, in various countries.

Some processed foods use the growth of micro-organisms as an essential production step. A wide range of products involve a bacterial fermentation process, including cheese and yogurt, sauerkraut, and salami. Here the process is essential to the creation of the flavour and character of the product, and contributes to its preservation and texture. Yeast fermentation processes are used to make breads, beer, wines and spirits. In fact, in all these products we can see biotechnology processes at work.

Currently about half the world's population eats its cereals in the form of porridge or gruel and about half as more complex products such as bread or chapatis. In developed countries bread consumption is in decline. In developing countries bread consumption is rising, in line with urbanisation. Commercial bread production can be traced in Egypt several thousand years ago. In the UK manorial or village ovens provided bread as long ago as the 11th century. In 1307 two companies were incorporated, the White Bakers and the Brown Bakers. In more modern times the pendulum has swung towards larger baking operations, and currently about 70% of all bread is produced by the major firms, operating very large and cost-efficient bakeries.

Breakfast cereals were developed in the USA in the late 19th century to meet the needs of religious groups, such as the Seventh Day Adventists, who were total vegetarians. The light, palatable and enjoyable products produced for this very restricted market by John and Will Kellogg found a much wider niche as social and environmental conditions changed. The trend has been away from heavy, calorie-rich, sustaining breakfasts towards lighter breakfast meals, and breakfast cereals found a natural market in this way.

This illustrates one of the realities of the food market. Food products only succeed widely when social change and changing consumer habits create a demand for certain food formats. The failure rate in grocery products today is very high. Many new products are not accepted by the consumer and disappear, and although advertising and marketing plays a big role in the industry, we must never lose sight of the fact that the major trends in food usage, in and out of the home, are much influenced by complex social changes in the family, in work and in individual situations.

The development of food preservation processes has, again, been a response to real needs such as:

- alleviating seasonal shortages
- feeding cities
- feeding armies
- providing food for travellers, explorers and even astronauts.

It is therefore worth describing why and how foods are preserved. The raw materials of foods, that is plants and animals from agricultural production, are vulnerable to spoilage and loss of quality from the moment of harvest or slaughter.

The tens of thousands of micro-organisms and moulds naturally associated with farm produce swing into action as soon as crops or animals are harvested or slaughtered, and this is a major cause of deterioration and inedibility in spoiled foods, together with internal enzymes which cause softening and bad flavours and odours (Figure 3). In addition, food poisoning hazards can arise in many foods from bacteria, such as salmonella, clostridia, staphylococci, campylobacter (and others), because these pathogens can come from the farm animals, from the environment, or from humans handling food.

In this context it is a worrying fact that the incidence of bacterial food poisoning outbreaks is increasing, mainly due to bad kitchen practices in the home and out-of-home eating. The modern preservation and packaging processes used in the food industry play a key part in preventing these hazards in manufactured foods.

Early man found various ways to slow or stop the natural degradation processes in foods. Typical examples include sun and air drying, heavy smoking and heavy salting. Removal or locking up of water prevents, or at least drastically slows down, both the microbial degradation and the chemical actions that spoil foods (Figure 4). Sun and air drying is still applied to fruits (raisins, sultanas, apricots, prunes etc) and also to some traditional fish products.

Use of dried foods has often been pioneered by explorers. Captain Cook, for example, took cakes of 'portable soup' with him on his major voyages. The lightness and transportability of dried foods are also major

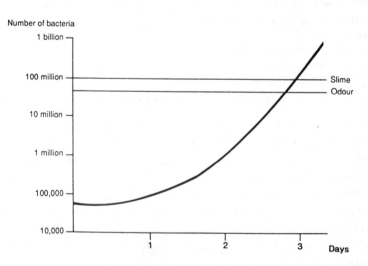

Figure 1.3   Meat at room temperature

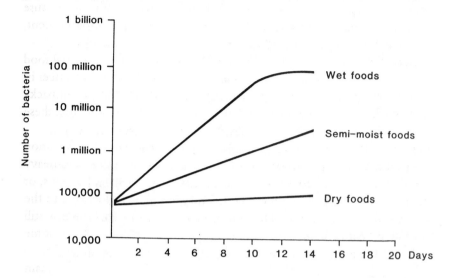

Figure 1.4   Effect of moisture levels on bacterial growth

assets in time of war, but some of the products developed in response to the spur of war have not enjoyed a good reputation, for example the notorious World War 2 dried eggs. In our own time, dried foods are of key importance in the manned space exploration programmes, both for their safety and diversity, and more particularly because of their lightness and compactness in terms of payload effect. For the rest of us, modern dehydrated foods provide a wide range of ready-to-use and attractive food and drink products.

Various processes are used: drying on heated drums, spray drying–where a spray of food or beverage is dried by warm air, or vacuum drying. All of these techniques use mild heat to evaporate water from the food. Milk powders, instant coffee and soup powders are examples. A novel method of drying involves extrusion cooking, which can be used to make breakfast cereals and snack products.

Another major food preservation technology originally stimulated by military need is canning. Napoleon, to feed his vast armies, encouraged developments in food technology and in 1810 Nicolas Appert won a prize for his novel process of preserving food using cut off champagne bottles in which to heat process the foods. An English merchant, Peter Durand, secured the foreign rights to Appert's patent and extended its scope to vessels of glass, pottery, tin or other metals. Thus was born the major convenience food technology of canning.

The whole aim of canning, especially of non-acid foods, is to totally destroy the micro-organisms and enzymes naturally present in and on foods, with the food being contained in robust sealed containers which prevent further external contamination. Figure 5 illustrates approximately the heat destruction of the spores of the most poisonous micro-organism, botulinum. This micro-organism occurs naturally in soil and water, and has heat resistant spores. If it grows in food it forms a deadly nerve toxin. Canned foods are submitted to high temperatures in a sealed can to make sure such heat resistant spores are destroyed.

Underlying this process is a lot of research. Careful experiments have

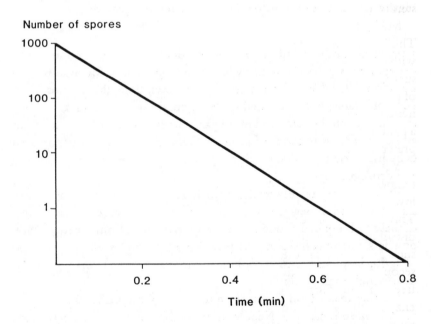

Figure 1.5   Botulinum destruction at 121° C

been carried out to measure exactly the rate at which the spores are killed at high temperatures. Then for any particular can size and product type, measurements and calculations are made to find out how fast all parts of the contents are heated. The modern sterilisation process is then calculated within a large safety margin to ensure that botulinum spores – if by any chance these are present in the coolest part of the can – will still be destroyed.

This process is usually carried out in large steam/water pressure cookers, with sophisticated controls and recording equipment. The super-tight seal on the can lid prevents entry of micro-organisms after sterilisation, and thus canned products have a long life. We should not forget what great convenience the ordinary can of food has provided in our daily lives.

Canning and sterilisation are not suitable for some foods which are adversely affected by the high temperature involved in this process. Milk is an example of a product where flavour changes occur in conventional sterilising.

Milder heat process – called pasteurisation – can be used in these cases. This kills the majority of micro-organisms, making the product safer and with better qualities, but all heat resistant organisms are not destroyed, and such products do not keep as long as sterilised products. Familiar examples of pasteurised products are seen in the milk and fruit juice sectors. Many items sold in the chill cabinet, such as some cooked meats, have undergone a pasteurising process to reduce the number of micro-organisms naturally present.

Yet another route to preservation with a long history, is to lower the temperature of foods. Again, because spoilage is of a biological nature, lowering the temperature slows the spoilage or even stops it altogether. This approach is used today in two rather separate routes of food distribution. One uses chill temperatures for relatively short term storage, such as you see on the dairy counters and delicatessen counters, and a second involves lowering the temperature much further. The whole deep freeze industry has been developed so that micro-organism growth and enzyme change are almost completely inhibited and foods can last many months or years in near fresh conditions (Figure 6).

Chilling has a particularly long history. Large manor houses had their

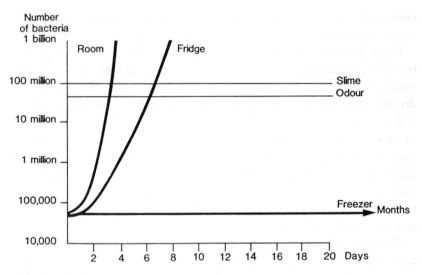

Figure 1.6   Storage temperature effect

own ice houses from the Middle Ages onwards, keeping ice for chilling products for long periods of the year. These were thick walled, insulated storage buildings, packed with ice cut from lakes and streams in the winter. Incidentally there was a thriving industry until early this century, in the northern states of the USA, cutting and exporting natural ice, sometimes as far as the West Indies. The Romans were doing the same sort of thing on a smaller scale for their banquets 2000 years earlier. The first successful commercial making of ice cream came into operation in 1875, and commercial refrigeration machines then drove out the harvesting of natural ice.

Chilling provides short term preservation, but it took the genius of Mr Clarence Birdseye, in the 1920s, to invent a process for deep freezing packaged foods. When a food is cooled slowly below freezing point the water in it freezes and produces ice crystals with sharp edges which can damage the fine structure of foods. The faster the food freezes, the smaller the crystals until you reach a point where damage to the food structure is avoided. It was Birdseye's achievement to exploit this *fast* freezing process. Quick freezing is carried out today by putting food packets in contact with very cold metal plates, or by passing them through a freezer tunnel where *very* cold air is being circulated.

Commercialisation of quick freezing began with fish fillets and spread to vegetables and other products. In recent decades, frozen foods have probably made the most important contribution to convenience and diversity of food provision since the earlier commercialisation of baking and canning. Frozen foods can provide complete meals, partly prepared meals or individual components, relieving the consumer of much of the handwork required in preparation, and as such are well in tune with the changing nature of modern lifestyles, as referred to earlier. The growth in quantity and variety of frozen and chilled foods has also depended on the technical improvement and greater availability of household equipment as shown by the growth of refrigerator and freezer ownership (Figure 7).

Drying, canning, chilling and freezing can be classified as physical modes of preservation, but there are some misunderstandings surrounding the use of non-physical methods of preservation. Salt with nitrates and nitrites are key food preservatives and have been used since Roman times in the production of ham and cured meats, sometimes together with smoking. Vinegar and other techniques of acidic preservation have probably been in use for just as long.

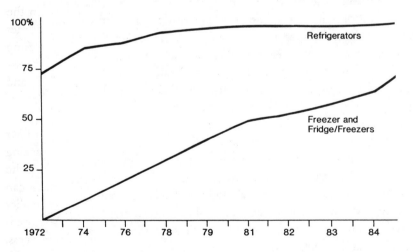

Figure 1.7 UK households with refrigerators or freezers

Similarly jams and jellies depend on a high sugar content to prevent water being used by spoilage micro-organisms and moulds, and have been with us for a very long time. These methods have all been applied in the more recent expansion of the food industry, as have other preservatives in order to slow the action of the many degrading enzymes and micro-organisms naturally found on foods.

Chemical preservatives such as benzoic acid, propionic acid and sorbic acid are naturally present in cranberries, Swiss cheese, and rowan berries respectively. These same chemicals are added as preservatives in some foods, but nowadays are made by the chemical industry rather than extracted from natural sources. These and other food preservatives are now strictly controlled by national and international legislation.

The application of technology to food processing has thus had a long history, but has certainly intensified in the last century with urbanisation, international food trade, and, in recent times, with substantial and steady social changes of all sorts affecting the way people wish to buy, prepare and eat foods. Equally, although food purchases are a declining part of average expenditure, sales of most foods have always been very price sensitive, and the pressure for more and more manufacturing efficiency for popular products has made the need for appropriate technology most important.

To illustrate the fact that technology plays many important roles in the modern shopping basket, one only has to look at a selection of day to day products from the supermarket shelf. An average selection of meat, fish, milk and other convenience products would show that these can only be made available on a large scale by the application of technologies such as canning, pasteurisation, UHT sterilisation, freezing, dehydration, vacuum packing, etc. These are the essential preservation systems needed for the safe distribution of these products.

Additionally, in the preparation of many of this diverse range of products, other technology steps have had to be used in the creation of products. For example, fermentation to make beer and lager, crystallisation processes to purify sugar, air-tight packaging to maintain the quality of instant dried products, high-speed filling and sealing for competitively priced canned products, controlled slicing for the wide variety of pre-sliced meat products, and so on.

These technical steps are used not only for the purpose of the manufacturer or the distributor, but to bring many and varied items of convenience to the consumer. From the same cross-section of a supermarket range, items of convenience for the consumer include longlife products, prepared cuisine recipes, pre-prepared complex sauces, robust canned products for convenient availability in the larder, single-use portions, such as tea bags or yogurt cups, instant products and many exotic food varieties.

FOOD ADDITIVES

Food additives have had a good deal of attention in recent times. However, a recent MAFF survey suggested that the consumer still does not have a lot of basic information, for example, why additives are necessary, what quantities are used, and how they are controlled. Consumers perceived additives, after fat, as the food ingredient most likely to cause a danger to health. It is, therefore, valuable to examine some of the facts about the use of additives. This area has recently been reviewed by Philip Strachan, when he gave a food scientist's view of the subject at a British Association forum last year.

Additives are natural or synthetic materials or compounds used to ensure that products are safe, that they are of reliable quality and attractive to look at and eat (Table 4). Additives used in industry are defined, tested and controlled, and fall in the categories shown. There are some 4000 of these ingredients which are permitted to be used. Some of which are additionally regulated by the EEC were given E numbers, which should have given extra assurance, but has been widely misunderstood (Table 5).Clearly, by far the majority of additives are flavours.

The comparative quantity of additives used can be seen in Table 6. Averaged over the population this means a total additive consumption per person of about 6lb p.a. Three pounds of this is made up of a few common ingredients used at a comparatively high level, the other 3lb consists of a large number of other additives, used at minute levels. The median intake of these minor additives is less than 1 mg per head per year.

On the largest category, flavours, very little is 'artificial'. About 43 000 of the 50 000 tonnes of flavours used in 1985 were natural ingredients. Another 4500 tons were made by reaction between natural ingredients

Table 1.4   Functions of additives

Main function	*Additive category*
Improved keepability	– Preservatives – Antioxidants – Sequestrants
Keepability and flavour	– Acidity Regulators
Improved flavour	– Flavours – Sweeteners – Flavour Potentiators
Improved appearance	– Colours – Glazing
Modified consistency and texture	– Emulsifiers – Stabilisers – Thickeners

Table 1.5   Types of additives

Additive categories	*'E'* *Numbers*	*No. of* *additives*
Colours	E100s	47
Preservatives	E200s	14
Antioxidants	E300s	14
Emulsifiers & stabilisers	E400s	56
Solvents		9
Sweeteners		12
Flour improvers		5
Flavours		c3 500
Miscellaneous		60

e.g.   gases
        humectants
        sequestrants		

before use. This leaves 2500 tonnes which are 'defined flavour substances'. Most of these are still purified extracts or 'nature identical' materials, so that about 17.5 tonnes are truly artificial.

Our total food consumption is about 40 million tonnes p.a., and is itself all chemical in nature, with many foods having natural components which would carry E numbers if we chose to add them in purified form (e.g. the natural lecithin in eggs would be E322, the natural yellow colour in milk would be E160a, and the ascorbic acid in citrus fruits would be E300).

Approval and control of additives falls under the 1984 Food Act, and depends on highly skilled and independent assessment of need and toxicological safety by the Food Advisory Committee and the Committee on Toxicology of the DHSS.

Finally, just to remind ourselves of the range of food hazards, the ranking shown in Table 7 is one with which many food safety specialists would agree, and was summarised in this form at the 6th Annual Marabou

Table 1.6   UK usage of additives 1985

Additive	Tonnes used
Flavourings	50 000
Flavour enhancers	6 000
Sweeteners	2 000
Stabilisers & thickeners	30 000
Acidulants	25 000
Emulsifiers	20 500
Colourings	11 000
Preservatives	2 500
Antioxidants	500
	148 000
Total food	40 000 000

Conference in 1978. We do public health a disservice if we do not keep this in mind when discussing food assurance issues.

PROCESSING AND FOOD NUTRIENTS

The major nutrients in food are usually not greatly damaged in factory processed or home processed foods. Heat processing can lead to a reduction in the levels of certain vitamins, in home cooking as well as in factory processing. Losses due to oxidation and enzyme action also occur during distribution and storage of fresh produce in shops and homes. Comparisons between foods and processing and distribution methods are very difficult, because of natural variation in the foods themselves. In the end, any comparisons that are attempted of processed and unprocessed foods should be on an as served, 'on-the-plate', basis. We also need to

Table 1.7   Ranking of food hazards

High Risk
1.   Microbiological Contamination
2.   Nutritional Imbalance
x1000
3.   Environmental Contamination
4.   Natural Toxins
x100
5.   Pesticide Residues
6.   Food Additives
Low Risk

(Source: 6th Annual Marabou
Symposium, Stockholm 1978)

remember that preserved products can and do deliver essential nutrients, out of season all year round. Overall, it seems clear that our food supply is delivering a sufficient level and variety of nutrients to the population as a whole.

LOOKING TO THE FUTURE

Looking at UK food consumption and to the future, it seems safe to predict that, as consumers, we will increasingly concern ourselves with the quality, the wholesomeness and nutritional contribution of the foods we eat. Social trends are likely to continue to put emphasis on convenience, and there is no fundamental reason for any major conflict between convenience and quality, including nutritional quality. There will be opportunities and pressure for more natural, less obviously processed and preserved, foods, and consumer buying patterns will reflect this. Food manufacturers will therefore be anxious to develop milder handling and processing options for foods, and there are examples, such as germ-free packaging of juices and dairy products, and the use of different shaped canned containers for certain products, which would allow milder processing, while maintaining the safety of foods.

Most households will be equipped with freezers and effective refrigerators, and therefore frozen and chill products will continue to play a major part in the shopping basket. Equally, kitchen preparation equipment such as microwave and multi-system ovens continue to grow in popularity and inevitably will affect consumers' choice of foods, and the design and packaging of products. Quick rehydrating beverages and other instant dried products will retain their popularity, since the convenient preparation by adding boiling water fits well within modern life.

However, it is important to emphasise that future change will arise from social changes in consumer cooking habits, eating habits, mealtime variations, family structures and availability of kitchen equipment. We will not see a future in which large numbers of completely novel or synthetic foods are successfully thrust onto the market place. Rather, we can anticipate a very wide range of products to meet the diverse requirements of a very diverse and complicated modern society. This will also lead to a further growth in specialised sectors of the food market.

Food manufacturers will continue to respond to consumer demand for products with special nutritional characteristics, but it should be remembered that a reduction in salt or sugar, or an increase in fibre in products, or a reduction of the enjoyable role of fats, can all affect eating satisfaction. Consumers will still insist on quality and attractiveness.

Technology will continue to be of assistance in meeting new demands with new products. Process technology can be used for the careful enrichment of certain foods with vitamins and minerals, or for the selective removal of components, for example decaffeinated coffee. Reduced fat dairy products, and low fat spreads both demand careful processing in their manufacture. Future food developments will call for more information about the structure of foods and the enjoyment of eating. Laboratory techniques will help us understand the complexities of foods.

Elaborately trained panels of tasters can help map consumer response to the physical properties of food, and this can also help achieve the best quality in processed foods. At all times we must remember that consumer choice will be based on millions of individual decisions which will affect the type and diversity of foods which succeed in the market place.

In food factories, more and more modern technology will be applied to the evaluation of raw materials and for monitoring processes to ensure that good quality products are manufactured at all times. For example, automatic television image monitoring is now available for monitoring the fat and lean ratio of meats being used in manufacturing, and this type of approach can be extended into many other aspects of quality control. Micro-electronics, as in other industries, will increasingly play a major role in the layout and management of food processing plants to ensure product quality and production efficiency. Computer-assisted quality assurance procedures will become widespread. Packaging formats of food will certainly continue to develop, to provide total protection of products and convenience to the consumer, with ready storage and easy opening and preparation.

The main preservation routes for food will continue to be freezing, chilling, canning and sterilisation, pasteurising, dehydration and semi-preservation. Key additives will still be necessary. Irradiation, which also kills contaminating micro-organisms, could be an important additional means of preservation. It certainly can provide some important advantages in the processing of certain foods, and is in use in several countries. It remains to be seen how widespread it becomes in terms of legal, manufacturing and consumer acceptance.

Biotechnology will obviously play a big role in and around the food industry, particularly because all our major raw materials come from biological sources. In selected areas, modification of food ingredients or production of food materials and flavours by biotechnology process methods is becoming more of a reality. It could well be that the food industry over the coming decades will also face many opportunities arising from changes in the nature of the raw materials coming from agriculture.

Biosciences applied to plants and animals should enable better economics of production. Cloning and selection techniques and even recombinant DNA techniques will enable more precise selection and development of crops and farm animals for quality and cost. This inevitably will open further options for the manufacturer in selection of materials to meet consumer needs of the time.

The future will also see continuing public and media attention to food issues. The issues will usually be many sided, and increasingly we should endeavour to strike a balance.

Yes – processed foods can be used to eat an unbalanced diet – but so can unprocessed foods.

Yes – some food processes lead to reduction of some nutrients – but so does storage of produce and home cooking.

Food processing is a wide range of procedures, many of them developed from kitchen arts and with a long history. The food manufacturing industry helps to provide a reliable food supply on a vast scale, which is safer than in any previous era. Food processing, of one sort or another, is an essential part of modern life. Today and in the future, consumers will be able to make many different individual choices to achieve a balanced diet, suited to their particular circumstances. There will certainly be a continuing need for more information about food. We all have a role to play.

Government will need to promote more awareness of its policies, procedures, and regulations for food. The 'Food Fact Sheets' issued by MAFF are an excellent start and should be extended. The food industry should increase its communication with the consumer about the role of food processes, and how quality and safety is provided for. The industry should also be alert if and when new technology makes it safe and practical to reduce the use of some additives, and be ready to make the changes.

Clear labelling should be used to explain necessary additives. Nutrition labelling in a common format is something that must come, and which is supported by industry. Imaginative and sympathic nutrition education will be required to get a wide and balanced understanding of diet and health relationships. With this growing availability of information, consumers should be able to avoid needless anxiety about food, while being better able to focus on particular issues of valid concern. Hopefully, the majority will also still enjoy their eating!

References

Industry & Food Consumption Details
Annual Report of National Food Survey, 1986
CSO *Annual Abstract of Statistics*, 1987 Edn
Social Trends 17, 1987 Edn

Additives
Strachan, P. W. *Food Additives*, (Unilever plc.)
Food Additives—(a) The balanced approach,(b) The numbers identified (Ministry of Agriculture, Fisheries & Food Unit, Alnwick, Northumberland)

2
Developments in agricultural biotechnology

P. G. BOSELEY

This paper covers two aspects which relate to 'Food production and processing'. The first is the direct improvement of plants by the application of new technology whilst the second addresses the possible replacement of agrochemicals using biological control agents.

IMPROVED PLANTS

Biotechnology will have a significant impact on crop plants in three respects:

(1) Product quality will be improved,
(2) Chemical inputs will be reduced,
(3) Crop yields will be increased.

Agriculture, over the past 50 years, has been very successful in increasing crop yields. Over half this increase can be attributed to plant breeding, the remainder to better agronomic practice and various chemical inputs. Although such yields need to remain high it is envisaged that biotechnology will aim at providing improvements to quality rather than quantity, and to productivity rather than total production.

The pace of scientific advance in plant breeding is accelerating as biotechnology offers new approaches to the plant breeder who for much of the past 50 years has had only conventional sexual crossing in his armoury. Biotechnology can supply new techniques which will increase the variation that the plant breeder can call upon. Such techniques include cytogenetics, tissue culture of haploids, somaclonal variation, protoplast fusion, genetical engineering.

Cytogenetics

The 'Alien Gene Transfer' or chromosome transfer technology has allowed the use of germplasm from widely related species to improve crops such as wheat. An example would be the transfer of a dwarfing gene from Bicornis, a wild grass, to Holdfast a bread-making wheat. The resulting products, Alien Dwarf 1, shows a much shorter straw length and the energy saved by the plant goes into the ears giving rise to a greater yield. Other genes which have been transferred in this manner have resulted in better bread making characteristics, resistance to fungal infections and tolerance to high salt concentrations. Interestingly, this technology of chromosome transfer provides a halfway house between the transfer of the whole genome and of a single gene.

Tissue culture of haploids

Anther culture, an example of this technology, allows the selection of specific desirable characteristics found in a particular plant variety and provides a route to fixing them. This 'fixing process' requires a doubling of the haploid number of chromosomes which are found in the anthers which results in the normal complement. The benefit of this process is that the time taken to produce new varieties is much shortened and in turn allows these new varieties to reach the market place quicker. This technique was used by the Rothamsted Experimental Station to obtain enhanced mildew resistance in barley.

Somaclonal variation

Protoplasts can be produced by stripping the epidermis from leaves and treating it with a mixture of enzymes. The resulting protoplasts can then be plated out onto media to encourage callus formation and shoot development. After shoots appear the callus is transferred to another medium which encourages root development. Finally the plantlets are placed in pots and grown up. During the period up to callus formation the genome reorganises, causing the phenomenon known as somaclonal variation. A classic example of somaclonal variation is the wide range of changes that can be obtained in leaf morphology with protoplasts from a single potato leaf. The practical benefit of somacloning in crops such as potato is that it reduces the time taken to bring varieties to National List Trials. For somacloning only 6 years is required rather than the normal 9–10 years for sexual crossing.

Protoplast Fusion

Protoplasts obtained by the same techniques outlined for somaclonal variation can be used to develop new plants by fusing cells from species which do not normally cross, for example, tomato and potato. Alternatively, cells from a particularly useful crop variety can be improved by fusing them with other varieties having associated beneficial characteristics. For the widely grown UK potato variety Maris Piper, possible improvements might include resistance to common scab (from Pentland Crown), foliage and tuber blight (from Pentland Squire), and cyst nematodes (from wild-type potatoes).

Genetical Engineering

The manipulation of specific genes, with a view to directly altering different traits within a crop species is an exciting possibility. This can be accomplished in a number of dicotyledonous plants by the transfer of a circular piece of DNA, known as a plasmid, which is found in a bacterium called *Agrobacterium tumefaciens*. This bacterium is known to cause crown galls in plants such as cherry trees and this observation resulted in its widespread use in a variety of plants to effect transformation. The plasmid found in these particular bacteria is called a Ti-plasmid, and using molecular biology techniques it can be manipulated to contain the gene of interest. The bacteria are used to infect a piece of plant tissue which is then grown up on different media to encourage first shoot and then root development. The resulting transformed plants can be tested for the existence of the plasmid DNA by assaying for particular genetic markers known to be associated with the plasmid. Using these techniques target genes are now being selected for use in the transformation of particular crop plants. These could include:

(1) Herbicide resistance genes, for example, the glyphosate resistance gene from Monsanto is now in field trials in tomatoes in the USA. This represents the first of many such genes which are likely to be introduced with the financial support of the agrochemical manufacturer.

(2) Insect resistance genes, for example, the transfer of the trypsin inhibitor gene from cowpea (black-eyed bean) into tobacco by the University of Durham and IPSR, Cambridge Laboratory. This inhibitor has a very broad spectrum of insecticidal activity and currently looks more promising than the much researched toxin gene from *Bacillus thuringiensis*. Although the cowpea trypsin inhibitor will be particularly valuable in cotton, maize and rice it will also be useful in such Northern European crops as oilseed rape. Such genes will result in a reduction in chemical insecticide use and will thereby have a positive environmental impact.

(3) Disease resistance genes. An example in this area is the virus resistance work taking place at the IPSR, Cambridge Laboratory on satellite viruses which promises to provide a mechanism of suppressing the symptoms of viruses such as cauliflower mosaic virus. Some of these viruses possess satellites which are small stretches of RNA. Such satellites can be of two types, virulent and benign, Virulent satellites produce necrosis in host plants whilst benign satellites attenuate expression of the symptoms by inhibiting replication of viral RNA. The sequence from a benign satellite has been put into plasmid DNA and used to transform plants. Such benign satellites expressed in these transformed plants prevent the expression of symptoms of virulent viruses and thereby prevents the onset of disease. It has been calculated for the US alone $1.5-2 billion in crop value is lost to viruses each year.

(4) Genes for key enzymes in intermediary metabolism, for example, cold-induced sweetening in potatoes. For UK food processors £4 million is lost each year in the cold storage of potatoes. This includes the need to spray anti-sprouting agents, fungicides and bacteriocides. Potatoes in storage undergo a sweetening due to the breakdown of starch to sugars in the tubers. The consequence for the crisp manufacturer is that on frying the potato a blackening occurs which result in an unpalatable flavour as well as the undesirable colour. This cold-induced sweetening appears to be due to the cold lability of one enzyme and this seems an ideal target for genetical engineering where the enzyme involved would be replaced with a cold-tolerant one. All these techniques are very interesting, but what about their direct application in a strategic way to improve crops?

'NEW' CROP PLANTS

Biotechnology will be brought to bear on a series of crop plants. Two receiving a lot of attention as a result of EEC subsidies are peas and oilseed rape.

Peas

In the EEC from 1983 to 1986 the area of field peas grown has nearly tripled and further increases are predicted for the future. This move into dry peas has been encouraged by the need for arable farmers to grow alternative crops to wheat and barley and for the EEC to become less dependent on imports of animal feedstuffs. Dry peas contain variable amounts of protein, lipids and carbohydrates and the Agricultural Genetics Company is seeking to produce peas in which the relative amounts of these storage products can be specified. In particular AGC is interested in:

(1) Characterisation of the R and Rb genetic loci known to be involved in controlling storage production composition,
(2) Increasing the genetic base for storage product quantity and quality through induced mutation and somaclonal variation,
(3) Genetic manipulation of peas and
(4) Improving tissue culture techniques for peas.

Oilseed rape

A huge increase in the EEC area of oilseed rape has resulted from the European Community aid scheme. The value of the EEC seed market for oilseed rape is currently about £25 million per annum. The main use of rape seed oil is for human consumption as salad and cooking oil as well as for the manufacture of margarine. Rape seed is also valuable for its meal which can be used, at low inclusion rates in animal feeds, particularly for cattle.

In conventional breeding programmes, varieties are selected for yield, oil content and quality, early maturity and for resistance to disease, lodging, pod shatter and sprouting of seed. This has led to varieties with high yield, improved oil and meal quality (ie. low erucic acid, reduced glucosinolates and low linolenic acid) and good resistance to stem canker and light leaf spot.

Because oilseed rape is amenable to tissue culture and genetic manipulation, there is potential to apply the techniques of anther culture, protoplast fusion and gene transfer for a rape improvement programme. The clearest opportunities are in:

(1) Anther culture linked to screening for quality characteristics;
(2) The production of F_1 hybrid varieties;
(3) Incorporation of virus and insect resistance by genetic manipulation;
(4) Genetic manipulation of other important genes.

DIAGNOSTIC TESTS

One area which is receiving far more attention following the advancement of new technologies is that of *diagnostic tests*. These are particularly useful for both determining and understanding diseases in crop plants. In addition diagnostic tests are becoming more prominent in the food production area where fresh foodstuffs are being tested for pesticide residues. A noticeable change has occurred so that even cans of beans at the supermarkets are becoming more detailed in listing their contents. Diagnostic tests will become more widely used in the future and their flexibility will be fuelled by further advancements in biotechnology.

BIOLOGICAL CONTROL

Biological control is unlikely to be competitive with agrochemicals in terms of price, speed of kill or convenience. However, the target markets for these products are niches which are not satisfied by agrochemicals. These would be where:

(1) The toxicity of residues is a problem with the chemicals;
(2) There are no effective chemical agents;
(3) There are secondary pest and disease problems resulting from the use of certain chemicals;
(4) Resistance to the chemical has occurred.

The pest and disease complex of crop plant has, in turn, its own pest and disease complex and certain members of this latter complex have been identified as potential biological control products. Three examples are, mushroom blotch antagonists, Cydia pomella granulosis virus, and insect parasitic nematodes.

Mushroom blotch antagonists

In the UK up to 10% of the mushroom crop is lost due to an infection of the mushroom cap with a bacterium called *Pseudomonas tolasii*. A group working at the Institute of Horticultural Research at Littlehampton have discovered some bacterial antagonists which are able to reduce the incidence of mushroom blotch by 50% or more. Such a biological control agent would be a good replacement for the only chemical treatment available, sodium hypochlorite, which is not effective.

Cydia pomella granulosis virus (CpGV)

This virus has been developed to combat the larvae of codling moth which affect orchards of apples, pears and walnuts worldwide. If organo-phosphates are used to control this pest a secondary problem arises from the red spider mite. Consequently CpGV is being investigated in conjunction with chemicals in an integrated pest management system. The advantage of this virus as a biological control agent is that it is highly specific to the codling moth larvae.

Insect parasitic nematodes

These nematodes are used for the control of sciarid, cecid and phorid fly larvae which can infest mushroom houses. No convenient chemical exists which is not either unpleasant or toxic to use by the growers or does not give residue problems in the crop. The insect parasitic nematodes possess symbiotic bacteria which are carried into the fly larvae when the nematodes enter the larvae via their orifices. The nematodes then penetrate the haemacoel of the larvae and inject the bacteria into it. These bacteria cause septicaemia and death of the larvae within 24 – 48 hours. The cadavers then act as a food store for the nematodes to multiply in and the offspring then migrate, locate and infect yet more fly larvae. These nematodes are a very effective biological control agent.

CONCLUSION

Although the paper has biased itself to mainly Northern European crops, biotechnology will affect and benefit crops and biological control problems worldwide.

Acknowledgements

I should like to thank my colleagues Peter Innes, Richard Connett and Fiona Paton for their tuition in agricultural biotechnology and my secretary Sue Kaufman for the excellent typing.

3
Novel foods
A. E. BENDER

Novel foods may be defined as anything that has not previously been eaten in quantity in the country in question. It becomes necessary to include these qualifications because some foods considered to be novel, such as moulds, yeasts and even bacteria have been easten in small amounts in most communities for many years. Questions of safety and nutritive value only arise if such foods become a significant part of the diet. The second qualification, namely 'in the country in question' is illustrated by the problem of favism. Broad beans are an acceptable food in many countries but not in the Mediteranean area and other countries where there is a common genetic defect.

LESSONS FROM HISTORY

There are several historical warnings from problems that have arisen, both from novel foods and from novel processes.

Maize, Saracen corn, was introduced into Europe in the 17th century and became an accepted part of the diet – part being the operative word. Crop failures and poverty in the early part of the 18th century in Spain led to much greater reliance on maize and so to pellagra, first called *mal de la rosa* by Casal in 1735. It is an intriguing example of the problems of scientific research to recall that Casal described the features of the disease and attributed it to the consumption of maize yet 250 years later pellagra is still a problem in areas where maize or sorghum is a staple food. After

47

going through the stages of ascribing the disease to a deficiency of protein, a deficiency of a vitamin, and the presence of a toxin we are still not clear how the relative excess of leucine in some sorghums plays a part.

An example of the problem resulting from a novel process is beri beri which first appeared in Japan in 1630 but only occurred occasionally. It became widespread in the middle of the last century when the introduction of steam-powered mills allowed large-scale replacement of brown rice by low-thiamin polished rice, and deaths reached a peak of 27 000 in 1923. This exemplified the point about the amount of the food in the diet – it matters little to us in the UK whether we eat our rice white or brown, but the problem arises when rice constitutes a major part of the diet.

Beri-beri, and similar deficiency diseases, disappeared where they did, not because deficient foods were taken out of the diet, nor because of enrichment with the missing nutrients, but because increasing prosperity led to a wider variety of foods in the diet, so that the shortcomings of the staple became less important. When beri-beri was at its peak in Japan a factory girl ate 600g of polished rice a day; by 1977 half of this had been replaced with other foods and the intake of thiamin increased from 0.7 to 1.7mg a day. Cases of beri-beri had become rare and usually due to excess alcohol consumption and poor dietary habits.

In 1974 several case of polyneuritis associated with oedema of the legs were reported in Japan, not in poor areas but among high school adolescent boys who actively engaged in sports. It was diagnosed as beri-beri, proven biochemically and cured with thiamin. Four hundred cases were reported from southern Japan in the five year period between 1973 and 1978. The diets were low in animal protein, 23g , and in thiamin, 0.6g per day, and were based largely on polished rice, soft drinks and sugar confections rich in carbohydrates. This experience demonstrates that even amidst relative wealth good nutrition cannot be taken for granted.

It is suggested (MAFF 1974 and DHSS/MAFF 1984) that any company intending to develop a new food or to market an imported one that falls within the description of a novel food should notify the Ministry (to evaluate potential changes in nutrient intake and safety). Such a suggestion should, presumably, also apply to novel processes, but that is not feasible. Extrusion cooking has been extensively studied, and some products marketed, but the process does not appear to have been considered in the same way as novel foods. Indeed it is not possible to define how extensive a change in processing must be before it is considered to be novel. The prime example is the discovery as recently as 1954 that vitamin B_6 is essential to human beings. A very small change in the processing procedure of infant milk formula, namely an increase in temperature, led to partial destruction of vitamin B_6 and to some 70 cases of convulsions in infants (Coursin, 1954).

NOVEL FOODS

The recent stimulus for the development of novel foods was the apparent world shortage, especially, it seemed at the time, of proteins. Whereas we now have difficulty in deciding whether famine is due to a genuine shortage of food or to a shortage of purchasing power, it was accepted in the 1940s and 1950s that there was not enough food in the world to feed the people of the world. It was even thought that while farming could fairly easily produce more carbohydrate foods the production of adequate supplies of protein foods was less likely, forgetting that two thirds of the world supplies of protein comes from cereals. The major problem in India today, for example, is edible oils. Little is available locally and some projected supplies are novel, including seeds from various trees not previously used in any quantities, various plants and from microorganisms. Rao pointed out (IDRC,1984) that the main interest now is in producing energy not protein.

There were in the early days of Food and Agriculture Organisation numerous ideas for utilising waste foods or converting animal feed into direct human food, growing highly efficient crops such as micro-organisms and using primary food sources at the beginning rather than the end of the biological chain. Such ideas arose from a variety of sources but for the purposes of discussion can be grouped as in Table 1.

Synthetic foods

We already make use of synthetic vitamins, additives and some amino acids but so far as we can see it is far easier and more efficient to grow the major foodstuffs than to synthesise them.

Table 3.1 Classification of novel foods

1 Synthetic:	Fats, vitamins, amino acids
2 Substitute foods:	Textured vegetable proteins, fabricated enriched wheat and rice grains, coffee whitener, mycoprotein substitutes, 'caviare' made from albumin, crab sticks
3 Primary food sources:	Plankton, krill, leaf protein
4 Microbiological sources	Yeasts, moulds, algae, bacteria
5 Upgraded animal feed:	Oilseed residues, fish meal, cannery waste, abattoir waste, seaweed

Substitute foods

A basic need underlying all ideas of novel foods, certainly for the vast majority, is that they must taste and behave in the same way as accepted traditional foods. Whatever advantages they may have in terms of price, yield, ease of harvest or consistency, the consumer will compare the new product with the well known accepted version. Many new, improved varieties of foods introduced over the years have failed for what might be considered trivial reasons, such as minor differences in colour, texture or cooking properties-despite acknowledged advantages. That is the problem with substitute foods whether they be textured soya intended to resemble meat, milk substitutes or, as introduced at one stage in India, formulated grains made from wheat and groundnut meal that simulated rice.

Primary foods

It is estimated that 10 000kg of plankton are needed to produce eventually 1kg of edible fish. So if we collect and consume the plankton directly there is a vast reservoir of food available in the seas. So far the energy cost of collection, apart from the lack of any technological functional properties of the plankton, puts this out of the question. However, in northwest Spain unusually high concentrations of plankton allow 'sea farming' of shell fish with speed and efficiency.

Krill, the small shrimp *Euphasia superba*, is said to have a potential of 50–100 million tons a year; over 20 years ago a mixture of krill and cheese was on sale in Moscow, and the shelled product is available in Chile. Considerable investigation into the ecological aspects is being carried out in the waters of south of Australia since krill is the food of certain types of whales and penguins.

Leaf protein can also be classed in this group. We cannot stomach enough leafy foods to make much contribution to the protein of the diet but the extraction of leaf protein, so closely associated with N. W. Pirie, would appear to open a 'new' source of a usable food. After 30 years of promulgating the idea it has not made much headway.

Non-food sources

Sawdust was used, at one time, as a basic material for hydrolysis to sugars and conversion to alcohol. Other examples are the suggested, and to a small extent experimental use, of wool and feathers as a source of protein.

Microbiological sources

The potential of micro-organisms is illustrated by the following: if one sets out with 1000kg starting material the daily yield would be 1kg from a steer, 86kg from soyabeans, 4000kg from yeast and 10^{13} kg from bacteria. One can add to the last example the fact that 50–100 million tons of gas are said to be flared off from the oilfields of the Middle East which could be the basic feed for such microorganisms.

A great deal of effort was put into the experimental work on growing algae, but was discontinued. The N-fixing blue-green alga, Spirulina, has indeed been used as a food in North Africa and Mexico for centuries and has even been promulgated as a source of vitamin B_{12}, as a slimming aid (Bender, 1985) and even as a source of protein (in 500mg capsules) in the western world.

Mycoprotein from mould has been marketed in the UK for the past two or three years. However, the problem of transforming this into food of a traditional type places the product also in the substitute group.

Upgraded materials

Fishmeal and oilseed residues are examples that have been investigated in depth. There is a large catch of small, bony and therefore inedible fish which is a very cheap source of protein and long used in animal feed. For about 25 years enormous efforts were devoted to rendering this fit for human consumption, in particular to removing the undesirable flavour and unwanted parts of the fish, and to maintaining the quality of the protein. Products made with 'fish protein concentrate' were demonstrated at the International Congress of Food Science and Technology in 1970 in Washington.

There were, however, three drawbacks, and these often apply to many other novelties. First, the extensive processing made a cheap material into an expensive product. Secondly, if the powder is intended as a supplement by incorporating into accepted foods, such as protein-enriched bread, there are usually cheaper materials available. Thirdly, the only other way to use a powder as a food is to spin, extrude or otherwise texturise it. This adds further to the cost and for which, again, cheaper starting materials are usually available.

So the efforts put into fish meal came to nothing. Oilseed residues were somewhat more successful; all that was needed was hygienic preparation, without too much nutritional damage, and such preparations are used to some extent in 'high protein weaning foods' where a powder is acceptable.

New or improved?

Very few foods can be labelled new, possibly only breakfast cereals and instant desserts were really new in their time, most other products were versions of known foods. This is certainly true of the new, improved varieties of existing plants and animals. Farmers first, then geneticists, have, for many years, been selecting new strains which fulfill a variety of requirements, and now the advent of genetic engineering will hasten the process and provide exactly what is asked for. However, they must, obviously, be acceptable to the consumer, who will compare them with products he has been used to eating.

When a working party of nutritionists and geneticists discussed new varieties of pulses (Hulse *et al.*, 1977) there was complete agreement that the first priority of any higher yielding varieties must be that they taste the same as those they replace (otherwise they would not be accepted). Since fuel is a major problem in many areas it was agreed that the second requirement of new strains must be ease of cooking. Nutritional aspects came only third on the list.

True novelty involves the extremely difficult problem of changing people's food habits. Many novel approaches have been suggested to augment food supplies in developing countries but it is more likely that novelty, if at all acceptable, would make an impact on an industrialised society which has modern communication and persuasion techniques, together with purchasing power. The popularity of previously little-known foods such as scampi, kiwi friut and avocados in Great Britain, together with more recent introduction from the south-east Pacific area of star fruit, rambutan, and even, in some limited parts of Europe, durian fruit, show that new foods can be made acceptable.

The introduction of foods from one community to another was explored in 1975 by a panel on tropical legumes (National Academy of Sciences, 1979). The particular interest in legumes lies in their enormous variety - 650 genera and 18 000 species - as well as in the ability of legumes to fix atmospheric nitrogen (at a rate of 500kg per hectare, which exceeds the world's total application of fertiliser). The panel circulated a list of 150 little known or neglected species, that seemed promising, to plant scientists around the world; more than 150 replied and added 250 further species. Thirty six were short-listed for detailed investigation including bambara groundnut, African yam bean, ye-eb (a shrub unknown outside the Horn of Africa, the nut of which has been eaten as their sole food by destitute Somalis) and grain amaranth. The last serves as an example of the potential of what is a novel food to the greater part of the world.

In pre-Columbian times amaranth was not only a basic food of the new world but the central feature of the religious and social structure of the Aztecs. With the collapse of the Indian culture, after the Spanish conquest, it fell into disuse (or, according to some reports, was deliberately destroyed to break down local culture) and survived only in small scattered mountain areas of Mexico and the Andes. The plant bears a crop of very small seeds, 1000–3000 per gram, containing 16% protein, which is more than that of cereals, and these contain twice as much lysine as wheat.

Since 1976 more than 1000 varieties have been collected and are under investigation to select those most suitable for various growing conditions. Already it provides a good yield of a useful product and is being grown by a small number of US farmers as a commercial crop, and is on the US market as a breakfast cereal. It has been introduced into Asia and is used as a form of bread in a few Himalayan communities although it contains little functional gluten. It is becoming popular in India where it is heated to expand like popcorn, and mixed with honey.

Amaranth leaves have been used in south-east Asia as a vegetable and are widely promulgated as a source of carotene to combat vitamin A deficiency. It is 'looked down on' as a vegetable in some areas, although the leaves are edible only 3–6 weeks after sowing the seed, and it can be cropped weekly for up to six months before finally being allowed to seed. Amaranth appears to have great potential although, of course, we have had miracle plants, and even miracle fish, before now that have failed. It took a century for the American farmers and the American public to accept soyabeans and two centuries for Europe to accept potatoes; on the other hand our commonplace peanuts and sunflower were not thought worthy of investigation a hundred years ago.

Safety testing

Safety testing of foods poses problems very different from those of additives, for which tests have been developed over the years. There is little to be gained from feeding large amounts of novel foods to experimental animals for long periods. It was pointed out by Hall (1985) that in the WHO Report on the *The wholesomeness of irradiated foods* half of the 53 animal tests that included a control group showed apparently adverse effects from the unirradiated food compared with stock diet. A similar problem would presumably arise if traditional foods and novel foods were subjected to the same type of investigation.

The problems were taken into account in three reports on testing the safety of novel foods, namely, *PAG Guidelines No.7* (PAG 1983), *Report on Novel Protein Foods* (MAFF 1984) and *Safety of Novel Foods* (IDRC 1984). The British Report pointed out that feeding trials can be planned only when detailed chemical investigation throws up problems of toxicity and nutritional value that can be identified. If feeding trials of the food itself become necessary the intended use of the food and the upper limit of its likely intake would be taken into consideration. For example, the protein quality of a food is not of interest if the food is not expected to replace a traditional source of protein.

It is generally agreed that each food must be approached as a separate entity and that there cannot be a standard protocol to cover all foods, and, obviously, much depends on the degree of novelty. One of the difficult problems is to determine whether the food causes intolerance and to compare this with traditional foods (for which some studies have shown that 5-60% of the sampled populations reported intolerance).

Ordinary toxicological tests are not effective in detecting such changes as behavioural (e.g. irritability), immunological modification (e.g. allergy), skeleto-muscular alteration (e.g. arthritis) and gastro–intestinal intolerance (e.g. associated with gut microflora changes) (IDRC 1984). It is pointed out in the Canadian Report that we are profoundly ignorant of the risks associated with traditional foods.

Nothing new under the sun

It is intriguing to note that many ideas for novel foods are by no means new. Biscuits enriched with fishmeal were made in Norway in 1880 and it was used as a flavouring agent in ancient Rome; leaf protein was first suggested in 1773; spun soya, intended to simulate meat, was a development of the 1960s but John Kellogg patented a substitute lamb chop made from wheat gluten in 1907. The modern technology of growing bacteria on methane and methanol was first carried out in 1906. Spirulina was discovered by Western science in 1970 but was known in Mexico for hundreds of years.

References

Abe, T (1982). A relapse of beri-beri in Japan. In Underwood, B. A. (ed.) *Methodologies for Human Population Studies in Nutrition Related to health*, pp. 185-92. US Dept. of Health and Human Services. National Institute of Health, NIH Publication No. 82-2462

Bender, A. E. (1985). *Heath or Hoax*. (Elvedon Press, England)

Coursin, D. B. (1954). Convulsive seizures in infants with pyridoxine deficient diet. *J. Amer. Med.Assoc.*, 406-8

DHSS (1980). Foods which simulate meat. Report on health and social subjects. No. 17. (HMSO, London.)

Hall, R. (1985). In Taylor, T. G. and Jenkins, N. K. (eds.) *Proceedings of the XIII International Congress of Nutrition*. pp. 816-9

Hulse, J. H., Rachie, K. O. and Billingsley, L. W. (1977). *Nutritional standards and methods of evaluation for food legume breeders. IDRCTS7e.* (International Development Research Centre, Ottawa, Canada)

IDRC (1984). *Safety of Novel Foods*. (International Development Research Centre, Ottawa, Canada)

MAFF (1974) Working Party on Novel Protein Foods; Nutritional aspects of those textured vegetable protein foods which simulate meat: In: *Report on novel protein foods by the Ministry of Agriculture, Fisheries and Food, Food Standards Committee* (FSC/REP/63) (HMSO, London)

MAFF/DHSS (1984) *Memorandum on the testing of novel foods. Guideline for testing by the advisory committee on irradiated and novel foods.* (Ministry of Agriculture, Fisheries and Food, London)

National Academy Press (1984). *Amaranth; modern prospects for an ancient crop*. Panel of the Advisory Committee on Technology Innovation. (National Research Council, Washington DC.)

National Academy of Sciences (1979). *Tropical Legumes; resources for the future*. Panel of the Advisory Committee on Technical Innovation. (Washington DC)

PAG (1983). *PAG/UNU Revised Guideline No.7; Human testing of novel foods*. (United Nations University)

4
Fruits and vegetables
J. D. SELMAN

The total sales of fruits and vegetables in the United Kingdom in 1985 were worth an estimated £4.1 billion. Fresh produce accounted for about 73% of this, canned products 16%, and frozen products 11%. The fresh and frozen markets have been growing particularly as a result of interest in healthy diets, and the efforts of retailers to widen the range of the more unusual and exotic produce.

The National Food Survey gives an indication of the relative consumption of vegetables and vegetable products in 1984, as shown in Table 1. (MAFF,1986). Potato consumption remained virtually constant during 1984 despite price increases, with consumption of fresh potatoes remaining dominant. Frozen chip consumption has now increased by 60% since 1980. Canned beans, peas and tomatoes, and frozen peas, comprise the major processed products. Table 2 indicates the consumption data for fruits and fruit products. Apples, bananas and oranges are the main fresh fruits and although overall consumption of these declined slightly, the consumption of fruit juices reached a record 5.28fl.oz. per person per week, representing a 70% increase since 1970. Thus vegetables comprise 33% of the total diet and fruits 11%.

The nutritional value of the vegetables as consumed is indicated in Table 3. Potatoes remain significant, not so much for their nutritional quality *per se*, as for the amounts consumed. Important amounts of

Table 4.1   Average UK household consumption of vegetables in 1984

	lb consumed per person per year	% total food per person per year
Total fresh potatoes	129.41	15.81
Total fresh green vegetables	35.20	4.30
Cabbage	11.90	1.45
Cauliflower	8.35	1.02
Leafy salads	4.91	0.60
Brussels sprouts	4.55	0.56
Beans	3.67	0.45
Peas	0.94	0.11
Others	0.81	0.45
Total other vegetables (fresh)	49.60	6.06
Tomatoes	12.28	1.5
Carrots	11.73	1.43
Onions	9.94	1.21
Turnips and swede	3.44	0.42
Mushrooms	2.37	0.29
Others	4.16	0.51
Total processed vegetables	55.02	6.72
(i) Non-frozen		
Canned beans	14.46	1.77
Canned peas	7.21	0.87
Tomatoes (canned & bottled)	4.35	0.53
Canned vegetables other than pulses, potatoes or tomatoes	3.44	0.42
Crisps and other potato products	2.96	0.36
Chips	2.24	0.27
Dried pulses	0.84	0.10
Canned potatoes	0.55	0.07
Vegetable juices	0.42	0.05
Instant potato	0.26	0.03
Air-dried vegetables	0.03	
Sub-total	36.76	4.49
(ii) Frozen vegetables		0.003
Frozen chips and other potato products	6.08	0.74
Frozen peas	5.53	0.68
Frozen beans	1.53	0.19
All frozen vegetables not specified elsewhere	3.74	0.46
Sub-total	16.88	2.06
Total vegetables	269.23	32.90

(Source: MAFF, 1986)

vitamins are contributed, as well as carbohydrate and minerals such as iron.
Table 4 displays similar data for fruits, with vitamin C being most notable.

FRESH PRODUCE

The nutritional value of fresh food crops has received much attention over
the years, with the quality of the raw materials as harvested being critical
to the product quality as consumed. Nutrient levels change progressively
through the stages of maturation, ripening and senescence. To maximise
nutrient retention it is usually necessary to handle harvested produce very

Table 4.2   Average UK household consumption of fruit in 1984

	lb consumed per person per year	% total food per person per year
Total fresh fruit	61.72	11.06
Apples	22.23	2.72
Bananas	9.46	1.16
Oranges	8.77	1.07
Other citrus fruits	6.01	0.73
Stone fruit	3.90	0.48
Pears	3.38	0.41
Soft fruit	3.12	0.38
Grapes	1.59	0.19
Rhubarb	1.30	0.16
Others	1.98	0.24
Other fruit and fruit products	27.80	3.40
Fruit juices	17.16	2.10
Canned peaches, pears & pineapple	3.83	0.47
Other canned or bottled fruit	3.57	0.44
Dried fruit & fruit products	2.76	0.34
Nuts & nut products	1.36	0.17
Frozen fruit & fruit products	0.1	0.01
Total fruit	90.51	11.06

(Source: MAFF, 1986.)

Table 4.3 Part of the nutritional value of some vegetables (as consumed)

| | % nutrient contributed to the average household diet | | | | | | | | | |
	Energy	Protein	Carbo-hydrate	Calcium	Iron	Thiamin	Nicotinic acid	Trypto-phan	Vitamin C	Carotene
Potatoes	5.0	3.6	10.1	1.3	5.9	8.4	10.7	4.8	21.9	—
Cabbage, brussels sprouts and cauliflower	0.2	0.9	0.2	1.0	1.1	0.8	0.7	0.4	6.2	2.4
Leafy salads	—	0.1	—	0.1	0.4	0.3	0.1	0.1	1.5	2.2
Fresh legumes	0.3	0.8	0.3	0.4	1.2	1.8	1.7	0.6	2.4	1.7
Other fresh greens	—	—	—	0.1	0.2	—	—	—	0.3	1.7
Fresh tomatoes	0.1	0.2	0.2	0.3	0.5	0.7	0.7	0.1	5.1	3.9
Carrots	0.1	0.1	0.2	0.6	0.6	0.4	0.5	0.1	0.6	55.5
Other root vegetables	0.1	0.1	0.2	0.3	0.2	0.2	0.3	0.1	0.9	0.1
Other vegetable produce	2.4	3.6	3.9	2.5	7.4	4.2	5.5	3.5	10.5	15.4
Total	8.9	9.3	15.1	6.7	17.5	16.7	20.2	10.1	49.5	82.9

(Source: MAFF, 1986)

Table 4.4 Part of the nutritional value of some fruits (as consumed)

	% nutrient contributed to the average household									
	Energy	Protein	Carbo-hydrate	Calcium	Iron	Thiamin	Nicotinic acid	Trypto-phan	Vitamin C	Carotene
Oranges	0.1	0.1	0.3	0.4	0.2	0.6	0.1	—	6.6	0.2
Other citrus	0.1	—	0.1	0.2	0.1	0.2	0.1	—	3.3	0.1
Apples & pears	0.5	0.2	1.1	0.2	0.7	0.7	0.2	0.1	3.8	0.3
Soft fruit	0.1	0.1	0.2	0.2	0.3	0.1	0.1	—	3.5	0.1
Bananas	0.3	0.1	0.6	0.1	0.3	0.2	0.3	0.1	1.4	0.7
Other fresh fruit	0.1	0.1	0.2	0.2	0.3	0.2	0.2	—	1.2	1.2
Other fruit produce	1.8	0.7	2.9	0.7	2.4	1.6	1.7	0.6	20.4	1.1
Total	2.9	1.2	5.3	1.8	4.2	3.6	2.7	0.8	40.2	3.7

(Source: MAFF, 1986)

rapidly and under cool conditions. All methods of harvesting cause bruising and damage, thus enhancing enzymic activity, and, for example, there has been no significant change in the ascorbic acid level of canned tomato juice since mechanical harvesting of tomatoes was introduced (Gould, 1983).

Wilting of leafy vegetables is a major problem since it is usually accompanied by a rapid loss of ascorbic acid, especially if the ambient temperature is relatively high and the ambient moisture in the atmosphere is low. Carotene is rapidly lost by oxidation unless precautions are taken during handling and harvesting. The main method of extending shelf-life of fruits and vegetables, and consequently of minimising losses of nutrients, is to handle and to transport the produce under low temperatures. However, avoidance of chill damage is needed for some produce: peppers, bananas and tomatoes, for example, sustain damage if chilled below 13° C.

The production of chilled prepared salads has been growing very rapidly, with coleslaw the favourite product. Slicing and shredding of vegetables causes loss of nutrients, and contact with other ingredients such as mayonnaise may cause further nutrient loss. For example, Figure 1 shows the effect of shredding cabbage and the effect of mayonnaise on the ascorbic acid levels of the product. Further testing, as yet incomplete, surprisingly suggested that acetic acid is the causative agent for vitamin C loss. Further work in such products is required (Hall,1984).

MODIFIED ATMOSPHERE PACKAGING

A significant development in chilled fruit and vegetable production is modified atmosphere packaging (MAP). While controlled atmosphere storage of fruits and vegetables has been used for bulk storage, such control may not be possible within a retail pack. Suitably permeable packaging films, however, may permit the development of an equilibrium modified atmosphere after closing, which results in the slowing of respiration and the extension of shelf-life. Unlike meat and fish, the harvested vegetables continue to respire and may exhibit a wide range of oxygen uptakes and carbon dioxide outputs. High respiration rates are usually associated with short storage life, and preparation of the raw vegetable by slicing or shredding may cause an increase in respiration rate. In general respiration rate will be influenced by cultivar, piece size, tissue age, storage temperature, damage, and atmospheric composition.

When oxygen supply is normal, aerobic respiration occurs, but if there is no oxygen only anaerobic respiration is possible. As the oxygen level is reduced, both processes function in proportion to the relative concentration of oxygen in the atmosphere. Hence a point is reached where a minimal aerobic respiration occurs with no anaerobic component. This results in a general reduction of metabolism and retardation of senescence or ageing. The optimal oxygen and carbon dioxide levels are dependent on the product and storage temperature.

In a sealed package containing produce, a modified atmosphere results naturally due to oxygen uptake and carbon dioxide production. Initially the concentration of carbon dioxide increases and the concentration of oxygen falls. If the film is permeable to oxygen and carbon dioxide gases, then as the concentration of carbon dioxide rises, carbon dioxide will diffuse through the packaging film at an increasing rate. Similarly as oxygen is utilised, oxygen will diffuse into the package at a rate dependent on the concentration gradient. Eventually an equilibrium is established when the

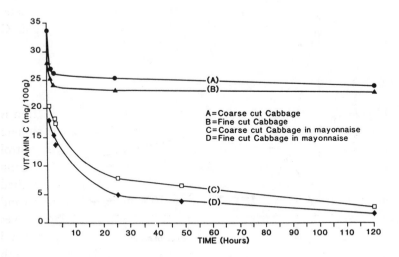

Figure 4.1 Vitamin C content of cabbage and the effect of shredding on stability. *(Source: Hall, 1984)*

rate of gas transmissions through the package equals the rate of product respiration. The actual equilibrium attained depends on respiration rate, fill weight, film permeability to oxygen and carbon dioxide, and the surface area for gas exchange (Tomkins,1962). This equilibrium can be allowed to develop naturally, or the pack can be flushed with the equilibrium atmosphere prior to closing.

Film permeability varies with thickness, temperature and relative humidity. The permeability required to achieve any one specific equilibrium modified atmosphere must be defined for each product at a particular temperature. If the permeability is too low, anaerobic conditions will result in the pack. If the permeability is too high, little or no atmosphere modification will occur. For example, the usual high quality life of Dominil strawberries is one or two days at chill temperatures whereas modified atmosphere packaging to achieve an equilibrium of about 7% CO_2 and 2% O_2 extended the retention of the flavour and texture characteristics for eight days at 5°C in the dark (see Figure 2). For high

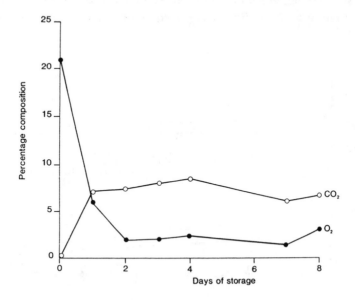

Figure 4.2   Strawberry pack atmosphere composition during storage at 5°C. (Fibre tray sealed with 25μm KLF film)

respiration rate products like mushrooms, further trials are being carried out to find films with high enough oxygen permeabilities greater than 44 000ml O_2 per m² per day per atmosphere (McLachlan and Stark, 1985, Ballantyne, 1986). Already some modified atmosphere packaged salad vegetables are on the market in the UK, and considerable investment in factories with chilled preparation areas has been made in France, for the production of retail and bulk packs of a variety of salad vegetables. To date little is known about the nutritional changes during storage in such packages.

FROZEN PRODUCTS

Frozen produce has increased in popularity because of convenience in home preparation, particularly when combined with microwave cooking. 98% of homes own deep freezers and 25% now own microwave ovens. Air blast freezing is the main means of freezing fruit and vegetables, with some use of liquid nitrogen for more delicate products. The small use of freon 12 for direct liquid immersion of delicate fruits like raspberries is now likely to be disallowed by the EEC.

Overall, it is the blanching process that precedes freezing which causes the greatest loss of nutrients, (by leaching and heat destruction), typically up to 40% for minerals and certain vitamins, 35% for sugars and 20% for protein. The blanching operation is required to inactivate enzymes that would otherwise cause deterioration during frozen storage. The most widely used type of blancher is the rotary water blancher, although energy consumption and nutrient losses may be higher than with the more sophisticated blancher designs now available (Selman,1987). For example, steam blanching minimises leaching and has been shown to reduce nutrient losses.

The principle of the ABCO K2 steam blancher is shown in Figure 3. A single layer of the vegetable material is exposed to steam for about 25 sec, in the heating unit, followed by about 50 sec (depending on the vegetable) in a deep bed to allow equilibriation of temperature throughout the vegetable pieces. The operational principle of the Cabinplant integrated water-blancher cooler is simpler than the ABCO as shown in Figure 4. The design is not unlike many pasteurisers used for heating and

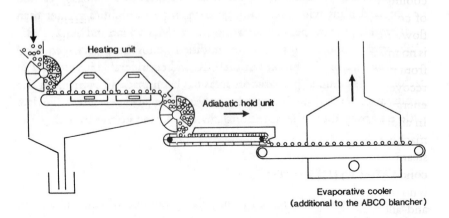

Figure 4.3   Diagrammatic representation of the ABCO K2 blancher.
(Source: Atherton and Adams, 1983)

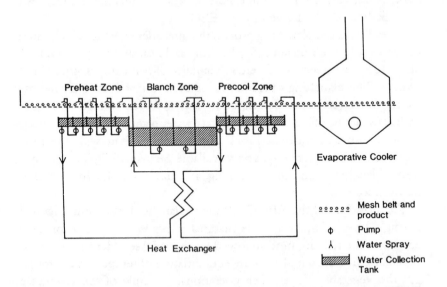

**Figure 4.4   Diagrammatic representation of Cabinplant blancher-
cooler.** *(Source: Atherton and Adams, 1983)*

cooling bottled products. Within the preheat and precool zones, a series of collection tanks and pumps are used to give a countercurrent water flow. These two zones are linked only via a heat exchanger so that there is no mixing of reheat and precool water, but there is a recovery of the heat from precooling. Basically, cold product enters and is heated by hot water recovered from the cooling product. There is therefore relatively little net energy usage once the system has been brought up to operating condition. In addition, because the highest temperature zone is in the centre of the machine there are very few evaporative losses. During operation, indirect steam heating is supplied only to the central blanching section, hot condensate being fed back to the boiler. Because of indirect heating there is no make up or overflow, further reducing heat loss and effluent volume, and allowing soluble solids to build up in the water, hence reducing leaching losses (see Figure 5). The lack of product movement during blanching and cooling should reduce product damage and help to increase

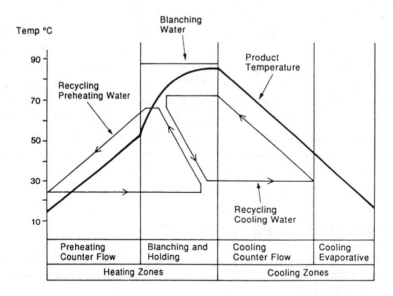

Figure 4.5 Representation of flow of water and temperatures in an integrated blancher-cooler with heat exchanger. *(Source: Atherton and Adams, 1983)*

yields. Currently in the UK little use is made of steam blanching, and there are only two or three Cabinplant blanchers in use (Atherton and Adams,1983).

A number of studies of microwave blanching have been carried out to explore the potential for reduced nutrient leaching, and rapid heating particularly for vegetables of large cross-section such as potatoes, corn on the cob, and brussels sprouts. On an industrial scale processing advantages have been identified: however, it was concluded that these were out-weighed by the high electricity costs. Until recently microwave genera-tors were limited to 30kw. However the development of 60kw generators which permit more uniform heating, and in combination with steam heating and humidity control to optimise efficiency, the cost effectiveness for blanching applications needs reviewing.

In freezing alone, losses of vitamin C rarely exceed 10%, and for most products are small (3-5%). Losses of vitamin B_1 are correspondingly low and carotene is relatively stable, with negligible losses in all products. During storage at -18°C the position is rather different. For example green beans and peas lose significant amounts of vitamin B_1, B_6, pantothenic acid and carotene after one year's storage. Most vitamins are sensitive to storage temperature and generally the lower the temperature, the less degradation takes place. At temperatures of -18°C or lower (-24 to -29°C in bulk stores), vitamins are more effectively preserved than at higher sub-freezing temperatures (Jul, 1984; Van Arsdel *et al.*, 1969). The application of time temperature indicators for use on retail or bulk packs may help root out packs that have experienced storage temperature abuse. In general freezing is often regarded as the best method of preserving vitamin components and other nutrients.

HEAT-PRESERVED PRODUCTS

Heat-preserved fruits and vegetables can be highly nutritious when processed in the best possible way and the typical operations involved are shown in Figure 6.

New fruit and vegetable cultivars are being evaluated for their suitabil-ity for processing because raw material quality significantly influences final product quality. Optimum harvesting time and growing conditions may

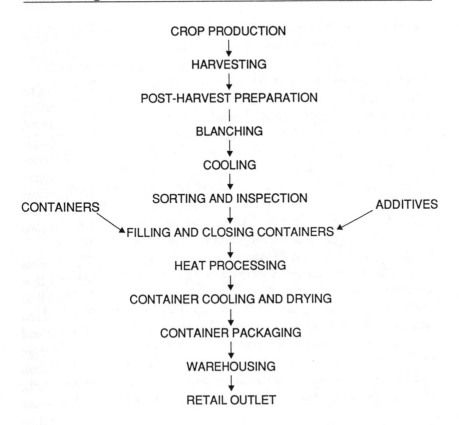

Figure 4.6   Flow sheet of the main operations in a canning line.

influence product colour, texture and flavour attributes, the nutritional composition and the level of contaminants such as pesticide residues. The design of harvesting equipment should minimise mechanical damage, transportation to the factory should be rapid, and raw material may have to be chilled to minimise post-harvest physiological changes that may result in nutrient and other quality losses. Preparation operations (similar to those required for preparing material for freezing) such as washing, peeling, cutting and slicing, should be efficient. The equipment for these should be routinely maintained to minimise waste and maximise yield.

A blanching operation may be required to inactivate enzymes if any significant delay is likely to occur prior to the heat-processing operation itself. However the objectives are usually to remove intercellular air from the vegetable tissue in order to reduce the oxygen content of the packed product, and to shrink the vegetable to help attain the desired fill weight. The most widely used type of blancher is the rotary water blancher.

Specialised blanchers for achieving a combined blanching and rehydration of dried vegetables have recently been designed to effect a one hour simultaneous soak and blanch at a suitable temperature.

Product acidity influences the severity of the heat process required. The spores of *Clostridium botulinum* are unable to germinate in products with a pH of less than 4.5 and so these may be subjected to a pasteurising process, whereas products with a pH greater than 4.5 must be heat treated sufficiently to destroy any of these spores which may be present. The pH of raw fruit and vegetables varies between cultivars and from year to year, and requires routine standardised measurement. Some typical pH values of canned fruit and vegetables are shown in Table 5. The artificial acidification of some products to permit the less severe pasteurising processes, may also result in improved nutritional and sensory quality. Several new products have recently been developed in the USA (Stroup *et al.*, 1985) Acidification procedures and the critical points are summarised elsewhere (Anon, 1979). Any nutritional benefits have yet to be evaluated.

Considerable developments in packaging continue. Retortable pouches and plastic tray types may have the disadvantage of slower filling speeds because of a lack of suitable handling equipment. However the advantage of processing in thin cross-section pouches is that less heat is required and hence shorter processing times are needed. With the larger packs having a maximum thickness of 2-3cm, nutritional and sensory quality should be enhanced when compared to the larger sizes of cylindrical container of comparable volume.

The tinplate food can remains most popular and has also seen recent developments. For example the use of tin-free steel (TFS) ends is increasing. Although these are most resistant to corrosion, they are harder and less malleable, and may cause more rapid wear of seaming rolls. Hence seam evaluations may have to be more frequent. The use of thin-walled beverage cans, to reduce container weight and cost, has been studied for the heat processing of fruit and vegetables under nitrogen pressure. Trial packs of raspberries, blackcurrants, green beans and beans in tomato sauce

Table 4.5   Typical pH values of some canned fruits and vegetables

Canned fruits			
Apples	2.9 – 3.4	Melon	4.1 – 4.3
Apricot	3.5 – 3.9	Nectarine	4.0 – 4.1
Blackberry	2.8 – 3.6		3.0 – 3.2 Orange
Blackcurrant	3.0 – 3.2		
Cherry	3.8 – 4.5	Pawpaw *	4.5 – 5.1
Damson	3.0 – 3.2	Passion fruit	3.4 – 3.5
Fig *	4.4 – 5.0	Peach	3.6 – 4.0
Gooseberry	2.9 – 3.2	Pear *	3.9 – 4.7
Grape	3.1 – 3.6	Pineapple	3.5 – 4.1
Grapefruit	3.2 – 3.8	Plum	2.9 – 3.5
Guava	4.0 – 4.1	Prune	3.6 – 4.1
Jak	4.1 – 4.7	Rambutan *	4.6 – 4.8
Kumquat	3.6 – 3.7	Raspberry	3.1 – 3.6
Litchi *	4.1 – 4.7	Redcurrant	3.0 – 3.1
Loquat *	5.0 – 5.1	Strawberry	3.4 – 3.8
Mango	3.8 – 4.3	Tomato *	4.3 – 4.7
Canned vegetables			
Asparagus	5.5 – 6.0	Eggplant	5.6
Beans in		Mushrooms	6.2
tomato sauce	5.3 – 5.9	Olives	6.9
Beans:		Parsnip	5.1
broad	6.0	Peas	6.0 – 6.2
runner	5.2 – 5.6	Potato	5.4 – 5.8
red kidney	5.9	Pumpkin	5.3
soya green	6.6	Sauerkraut	3.5
Beetroot	5.2 – 5.5	Spinach	5.4 – 6.0
Carrot	5.1 – 5.3	Swede	4.7 – 5.1
Cauliflower	5.7 – 6.1	Turnip	5.5
Corn	6.1 – 6.3		

* May require acidification for safe processing;
  cultivars should be checked.
(Source: Holdsworth, 1983)

have been successfully produced in this manner, although nutritional evaluation has not yet been included (Gaze and Selman,1987).

In addition to the prepared fruit or vegetables, a suitable brine, syrup or sauce may be required to be prepared and filled into the container. It is essential that all these should be prepared within the specified requirements and recipes, because factors such as vegetable piece dimensions, syrup viscosities, concentration of thickeners, their temperatures and the solids to liquid ratios, may all affect the heating characteristics of the pack during processing. This in turn will influence the achievement of a sterile product and the degree of cooking.

Filling must be carefully controlled to prevent material wastage and strong effluents, and the formation of a poor seam. The headspace must be carefully controlled since this affects the heating behaviour of the can, particularly during agitated processing. The final vacuum in the can will also be influenced (typically about 8 in. Hg or 0.27 bar if the cans are closed at 60°C), and the potential for can damage by peaking or panelling. Filling rates vary from about 300-600 cans per minute typically, and UK manufacturers aim to achieve specified minimum *filled weights* for prepared fruit and vegetables in the various can sizes, and the minimum total solids for dried vegetable packs (BFVCA, 1986). Currently the European Economic Community (EEC) legislative harmonisation programme intends that the basis of trading in the canning industry should be changed from this code of practice to a system of *drained weights* of produce, measured at least 30 days after manufacture. This poses certain problems as drained weights may be more variable than filled weights, and depend upon factors such as cultivar, maturity, preparation procedures, peeling, syrup stength, filling equipment and speeds, and processing and storage ·conditions (Atherton, 1975).

Scheduled heat process times and temperatures have been determined experimentally for many fruit and vegetable products in various can sizes, under static and agitated conditions (Atherton and Thorpe, 1980). The achievement of microbiologically stable products is dependent on the good manufacturing practices associated with all the related operations, from preparation procedures to post-process cooling and handling. Batch retorts offer great flexibility regarding pack type and size, and a number of new designs are available, including water retorts, incorporating overpressure for glass and plastic containers, Steriflow retorts that utilise an external heat exchanger to heat and cool the process water indirectly, and steristeam steam/air mixture retorts. Most of these retorts can be linked to automatic handling equipment.

The prime objective of heat preservation is to stabilise and preserve the product by inactivating microorganisms and enzyme systems. At the same time it is necessary to minimise nutrient loss both during processing and subsequent storage and achieve desirable sensory quality, (Priestley, 1979; Labuza, 1982). The ability to optimise these changes requires kinetic data for the various thermal effects, thus enabling prediction of nutrient loss resulting from given process conditions. These are well reviewed elsewhere (Holdsworth, 1985; Leonard *et al.*, 1986).

Retention of the quality of some of the delicate tropical fruits has been improved by can spinning systems within retorts to improve the rate of heat transfer and reduce process time. Flame sterilization, although not widely used, is a technique for high temperature short time processing which gives improved product quality (reviewed by Richardson, 1987). Microwave processing systems are now being developed for in-pack pasteurisation processes and eventually may be capable of rapid sterilization processes (CFPRA, 1986). At the Campden Food R.A., research is being carried out on the continuous heat processing, followed by aseptic packaging, of fluids containing low-acid food particulates including vegetable pieces (Holdsworth and Nos, 1982).

The advantages of these high temperature short time processes are illustrated in Figure 7 which shows the differing destruction kinetics of microorganisms and spores, and other cooking changes. Thus at higher temperatures (and consequently shorter process times) sterile product can be obtained with reduced losses of nutrients and sensory quality. For example, Figure 8 shows the levels of thiamin in retorted canned (250°F for 45 min) and aseptically packed canned carrots (300°F for 8 sec). One day after canning, the aseptically canned carrots contained 13µg thiamin per 100g sample, and the retorted product 4.8µg per 100g. During storage, thiamin content decreased slightly, and more rapidly at the higher temperature. The aseptic samples remained higher in thiamin content than the retorted samples (Luh *et al.*, 1969). Developments in heating systems and filling heads are advancing, and aseptically packed products containing

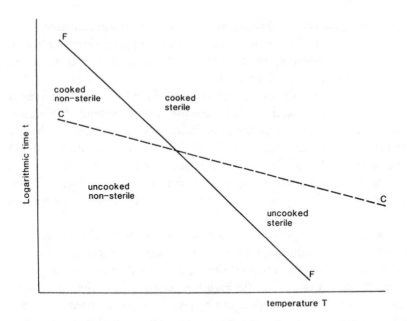

Figure 4.7   Diagram of t–T relationship for microbial destruction, F, and cooking, C. *(Source: Holdsworth, 1985)*

vegetable pieces up to 15mm, such as tomato and mushroom, are now available in soups and similar products. Large particle dispensing of vegetable and other pieces in the 20–25mm range is being developed now to permit the aseptic packing of prepared meals.

CHEMICAL PRESERVATIVES

The proportion of dehydrated fruit and vegetable products consumed is small (MacCarthy, 1986). However the use of sulphites, to minimise undesirable quality changes, such as browning during drying and as a preservative, has been widespread for several fruit and vegetable products (Taylor *et al.*, 1986). Usage has decreased in favour of an additive-free technology, for example, most fruit juice concentrates are now frozen rather than sulphited. Thiamin is easily destroyed by sulphites, and their use in the form of sprays for maintaining freshness of salads has caused

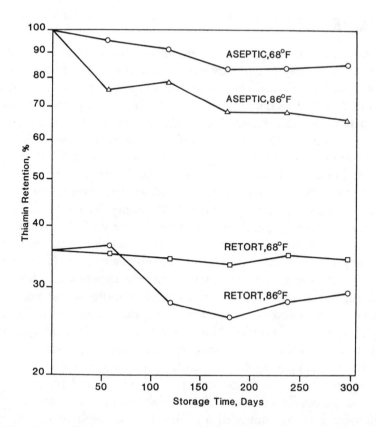

Figure 4.8 **Thiamin retention in retorted, canned (250°F, 45min), and aseptically packed canned carrots (300°F, 8sec), stored at 68 or 86°F.** *(Source: Lu et al., 1969)*

concern both for the levels present in the food as well as for sulphite-sensitive individuals (Anon, 1986).

The expansion in demand for pre-packed vegetables has led to an increase in the numbers of UK farmers and growers who process and pack their own produce for direct sale through retail outlets. For example beetroot may be dipped in acetic acid, or may be cooked and dipped in benzoic acid prior to pre-packing (Board et al., 1987). Overall this sector of the market remains small.

IRRADIATION

As heating is not induced by the use of ionising irradiation for food preservation, it may be necessary to inactivate enzymes in certain foods, using a suitable heat treatment. In general nutrient alteration in radiation processed foods does not differ much from that in heat processed foods. Comparatively, most vitamins behave differently towards heat and radiation, but vitamins with a low radiostability are usually susceptible to some other agent such as oxygen (Josephson, *et al.*, 1978). Biochemical changes may be induced, causing flavour, texture and other sensory changes, which may limit the application of irradiation to various foodstuffs, depending on their sensitivity (Moy, 1983). Some likely applications of irradiation reflect foodstuffs which are tolerant to undesirable changes, and those foods that have a market value high enough to withstand costs that may be additional to conventional processing costs (assuming a suitable cost-effective conventional technique is already available).

Ideally, irradiation is best applied to a simple, non-living host, contaminated with a genetically complex target organism. The control of *Trichina* in pork approaches this ideal. However the control of mould on living fruits and vegetables is less promising because the target organism is a simpler form of life than the host. Surface treatment with electrons may be the more appropriate irradiation process here. The delay of natural ripening and growth cannot be selectively altered by irradiation, whereas techniques such as controlled and modified atmosphere storage are designed to slow respiration of fruits and vegetables as discussed previously. Also plant growth hormones can have very specific effects.

Although a 2.4kGy dose can inhibit mould growth for 30 days in strawberries stored at 4°C, the effect is meaningless commercially without consideration of the time related changes in sensory quality. These quality requirements must be clearly defined, and some cultivars may be more tolerant to undesirable effects than others. A comparison of the effectiveness of mould control by various techniques is shown in Table 6 (Maehler, 1985).

Combination processes have been shown to be more effective in some cases than just irradiation alone. For example a five minute hot water dip in the fungicide Benlate combined with 0.75kGy irradiation has been shown to be the most effective treatment for mould inhibition in mangoes as shown in Figure 9 (Brodrick and Thomas, 1977). Similarly the combination of irradiation and modified atmosphere packaging may prove to be successful for some products.

In the United Kingdom irradiated foodstuffs are not permitted, and debate continues to surround a recent report to the UK government which was satisfied that ionising radiation up to an overall average dose of 10kGy, when correctly applied, can provide safe wholesome foods (ACINF, 1986). Meanwhile attention is being given to establishing codes of practice at an international level, and to developing standard tests to detect if foods have been irradiated.

Table 4.6   Mould control by various processes

Process	Reduce initial innoculum	Provide residual protection	Differential tolerance/ specificity rating	Overall rating[a]
Refrigeration	−	+	+ b	+
CA Storage	+	− c	+ b	+
MA Packaging	−	+ d	+ b	+
Fungicide/hot water	+	+ e	+ f	++
Fumigation	+	−	−	−
Irradiation	+	−	− g	−

a. This rating addresses technical aspects only and does not include practicality and economic assessments.
b. Some fruits are susceptible, but effects are generally desirable.
c. Protected only until release from store.
d. Relies on selective permeability of packaging.
e. Surface waxes can include fungicides for residual protection.
f. Specific to the surface only.
g. The dose required to induce the desired effect is often at least or more than the critical dose that induces undesirable effects.

(Source: Maehler 1985)

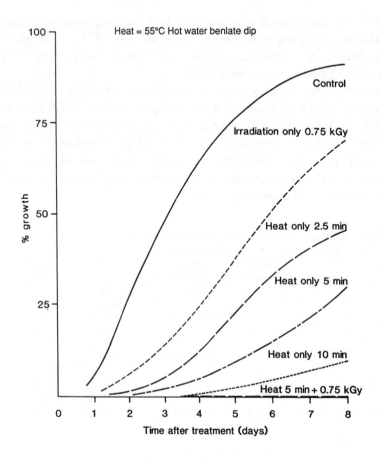

Figure 4.9   Fungal growth in mangoes *(Source: Brodrick and Thomas 1977)*

NUTRITIONAL COMPOSITION OF FRESH AND PROCESSED FOODS

It is not easy to make generalised comparisons between the nutritional composition of fresh and processed fruits and vegetables (Harris and Karmas, 1975; Tannenbaum, 1979; Bender, 1966). Some new data have been obtained, but the significance of the results is not easily assessed due to the many variable factors influencing nutrient content, such as cultivar, preparation and processing procedures, analytical techniques and the method of serving on the plate (Dudek *et al.*, 1982; Howlett, 1987). More data is required to assess the nutritional implications of the boom in domestic use of microwave ovens (Hill, 1981).

Some recent work at the Campden Food Preservation Research Association suggests that most changes in bulk components of fruit and vegetables result from water uptake or loss from the material, and so appear to be closely related to the cooking liquor. Leaching losses of several minerals have been observed, although sodium and calcium levels generally *increase* by uptake from process waters and brines. Vitamin C levels change most significantly, with losses on processing and cooking as shown in Table 7 (Bender, 1987). During storage of canned or frozen material, vitamin content remains fairly constant for most products.

An indication of the problems surrounding comparison of fresh and processed materials is illustrated in Figure 10, which shows the changing vitamin C content of peas with maturity. The optimum harvesting

Table 4.7   Vitamin C losses in vegetables during household cooking

	Vitamin C (%)		
Method	*Destroyed*	*Extracted*	*Retained*
GREEN VEGETABLES			
Boiling (long time, much water)	10 – 15	45 – 60	25 – 45
Boiling (short time, little water)	10 – 15	15 – 30	55 – 75
Steaming	30 – 40	<10	60 – 70
Pressure cooking	20 – 40	<10	60 – 80
ROOT VEGETABLES (unsliced)			
Boiling	10 – 20	15 – 25	55 – 75
Steaming	30 – 50	<10	50 – 70
Pressure cooking	44 – 55	<10	45 – 55

(Source: Bender, 1987)

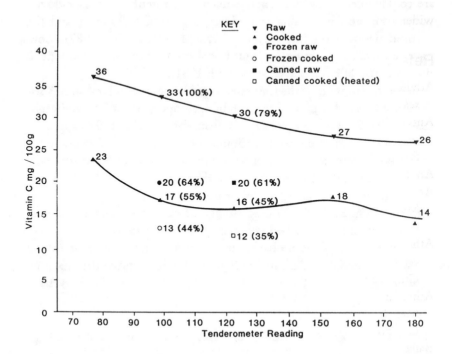

Figure 4.10   The relationship between vitamin C content and tender-ometer reading in peas *(Source: Hall, 1987)*

maturity for freezing peas is around a tenderometer reading of 95–100, whereas for canning it would be about 120+. The various processing and serving operations will influence vitamin C content, and the net vitamin C content of frozen or canned peas, as served on the plate, could well be the same (Hall, 1987).

Where there is a clear association of raw material maturity and/or storage with vitamin C levels, this may imply that the processing of a raw material in prime condition can result in the availability, out of season, of a product on the plate which has a vitamin C retention comparable to that of the cooked fresh equivalent in season. It might, therefore, reasonably be concluded that the many current material and process developments are contributing both to the improvement of nutritional value and to a wider choice of fruit and vegetable products for the consumer.

References

Advisory Committee on Irradiated and Novel Foods (1986). *Report on the safety and wholesomeness of irradiated foods.* (HMSO, London)

Anon. (1979). Acidified foods and low-acid canned foods in hermetically sealed containers. Emergency permit control and current good manufacturing practice. *Federal Register* 44, 16204-38

Anon (1986). Sulfites as food ingredients. *Food Technol.,* 40, (6), 47-52

Atherton, D. (1975). *The drained weights of canned fruits and vegetables.* Tech. Memo. No. 146 (Campden Food Preservation R.A., Chipping Campden)

Atherton, D. and Thorpe, R. H. (1980). *The processing of canned fruit and vegetables.* Tech. Bull. No. 4. (Campden Food Preservation R.A., Chipping Campden)

Atherton, D. and Adams, J. B. (1983). *New blanching systems.* Tech. Memo. No. 319. (Campden Food Preservation R.A., Chipping Campden)

Ballantyne, A. (1986). *Modified atmosphere packaging of selected prepared vegetables.* Tech. Memo. No. 436. (Campden Food Preservation R.A., Chipping Campden)

Bender, A. E. (1966). Nutritional Effects of Food Processing. *J. Food Technology,* 1. 261-89

Bender, A. E. (1987). Nutritional changes in food processing. In Thorne, S. (ed.) *Developments in Food Preservation* Vol. 4. pp. 1-34. (Elsevier Applied Science, London)

BFVCA (1986). *Code of practice on canned fruit and vegetables.* (British Fruit and Vegetable Canners Association, London)

Board, R. G., Allwood, M. C. and Banks, J. G. (1987). *Preservatives in the food, pharmaceutical and environmental industries.* (Blackwell Scientific Publications, Oxford)

Brodrick, H. T. and Thomas, A. C. (1977). Radiation preservation of sub-tropical fruits in South Africa. In *Food preservation by irradiation.* Vol. 1. pp. 167-78. (International Atomic Energy Agency, Vienna)

CFPRA (1986). *Microwave and resistance heating for the food industry.* Symposium Proceedings 27th November, 1986. (Campden Food Preservation R. A., Chipping Campden)

Dudek, J. A., Elkins, E. R, Chin, H. and Hagen. R. (1982). *Investigations to determine nutrient content of selected fruits and vegetables - raw, processed and prepared.* (National Food Processors Association, New York)

FAO (1981). *Improvement of nutritional quality of food crops.* FAO Plant and Protection Paper 34. (Food and Agriculture Organisation of the United Nations, Rome)

Gaze, R. R. and Selman, J. D. (1987). *The use of thin-walled cans pressurised by the injection of liquid nitrogen for packaging processed foods.* Part II Tech. Memo. No. 439. (Campden Food Preservation R.A., Chipping Campden)

Gould, W.A. (1983). *Tomato production, processing and quality evaluation.* (AVI Publishing Co., Westport, USA)

Hall, M. N. (1984). Interim Report: *Chemical changes occurring in chilled foods* (P1331). (Campden Food Preservation Research Association, Chipping Campden)

Hall, M. N. (1987). Personal communication, Department of Chemistry and Biochemistry, Campden Food Preservation, R.A., Chipping Campden

Harris, R. S. and Karmas, E. (eds) (1975). *Nutritional evaluation of food processing.* 2nd edn. (AVI Publishing Co., Westport, USA)

Hill, M. A. (1981). The effect of microwave processing on the chemical, physical and organoleptic properties of some foods. In Thorne, S. (ed.) *Developments in food processing* Vol. 1. pp. 121-51. (Applied Science, London)

Holdsworth, S. D. and Nos, S. N. (1982). *Food particle sterilization.* Tech. Memo. No. 287. (Campden Food Preservation R.A., Chipping Campden)

Holdsworth, S. D. (1983). *The preservation of fruit and vegetable food products.* (Macmillan Press, London)

Holdsworth, S. D. (1985). Optimisation of thermal processing-a review. *J. Food Eng.* 4, 89-116

Howlett, M. C. (1987). *A critical review of recent literature on the effects of processing on the composition of vegetables.* Tech. Note. No. 174. (Campden Food Preservation R. A., Chipping Campden)

Josephson, E. S., Thomas, M. H. and Calhoun, W. K. (1978). Nutritional aspects of food irradiation. *J. Food Proc. Pres.*, 2, 299-313

Jul, M. (1984). *The quality of frozen foods*. (Academic Press, London)

Labuza, T. P. (1982). *Shelf-life dating of foods*. (Food Nutrition Press, Westport, USA)

Leonard, S. J., Merson, R. L., Marsh, G. L. and Heil, J. R. (1986). Estimating thermal degradation in processing of foods. *J. Agric. Food Chem.*, 34, 392-6

Luh, B. S., Antonakos, J. and Daoud, H. N. (1969). Chemical and quality changes in strained carrots by the aseptic and retort processes. *Food Technol.*, 23, 103

Maehler, R. (1985). Which foods? In *Irradiated foods: a new business*, pp. 3-13. (The Food Processors Institute, Washington DC)

MacCarthy, D. (ed). (1986). *Concentration and drying of foods*. (Elsevier Applied Science, London)

MAFF (1986). *Household food consumption and expenditure in 1984*. Annual Report of the National Food Survey Committee. (HMSO, London)

McLachlan, A. and Stark, R. (1985). *Modified atmosphere packaging of selected prepared vegetables*. Tech. Memo. No. 412. (Campden Food Preservation R.A., Chipping Campden)

Moy, J. H. (1983). Radurization and radicidation: fruits and vegetables. In Josephson, E. S. and Peterson, M. S. (eds.) *Preservation of food by ionizing radiation*. Vol III, pp. 83-108. (CRC Press, Florida, USA)

Peleg, K. (1985). *Produce handling, packaging and distribution*. (AVI Publishing Co., Westport, USA)

Priestley, R. J. (ed). (1979). *Effects of heating on foodstuffs*. (Applied Science Publishers, London)

Richardson, P. S. (1987). Flame Sterilization. *International J. Food Sci. Technol.* 22, 3-14

Schuphan, W. (1965). *Nutritional value of food crops and plants*. (Faber and Faber, London)

Selman, J. D. (1987). The Blanching Process. In Thorne, S. (ed.) *Developments in food preservation*, Vol. 4. (Elsevier Applied Science, London)

Stroup, W. H., Dickerson, R. W. and Johnston, M. R. (1985). Acid equilibrium development in mushrooms, pearl onions and cherry peppers. *J. Food Protection*, 48, 590-4

Tannenbaum, S. R. (1979). *Nutritional and safety aspects of food processing.* (Marcel Dekker, New York)

Tomkins, R. G. (1962). The conditions produced in film packages by fresh fruit and vegetables and the effect of these conditions on storage life. *J. Appl. Biol.*, 25, 290-307

Taylor, S. L., Higley, N. A. and Bush, R. K. (1986). Sulfites in foods: uses, analytical methods, residues, fate, exposure assessment, metabolism, toxicity and hypersensitivity. *Adv. Food Res.*, 30., 1-76

Van Arsdel, W. B., Copley, M. J. and Olson, R. L. (1969). *Quality and stability of frozen foods.* (Wiley Interscience, New York)

Woodroof, J. G. and Luh, B. S. (1986). *Commercial fruit processing.* 2nd edn. (AVI Publishing Co., Westport. USA)

5
Cereals and cereal products
B. SPENCER

The cultivation of wild wheat grasses *(Triticum boeticum)* and wild barley *(Hordein spontaneum)*, and subsequently the selection of plants that could be harvested and threshed easily, such as Einkorn and Emmer, was the crucial step in facilitating the change of man from a wandering nomad and hunter to a settler. Food availability was no longer restricting population growth and centres of civilisation, starting in Sumer, Ur and Babylon, based on adequate cereal food supplies, became feasible.

True bread wheats as we recognise them today, of the type *Triticum aestivum*, derived from Emmer crossed with wild grasses, developed shortly afterwards but the bread baked by the ancients was hardly the bold, well-risen loaf of today. Rather it was dense, coarse in texture, dark in colour, flat and unleavened. The nearest modern day equivalent is the chappati or shrak, from Jordan, which is a pancake of wholemeal, baked in a stove, and looks like a piece of calico.

The art of breadmaking received a boost in ancient Egypt, whose civilisation and culture were based on the ample harvests of wheat grown on the rich alluvial delta lands. Wheat was ground by the primitive technique of rubbing grain on a saddlestone with a muller but the Egyptians improved on the baking of bread on hot stones by inventing the oven, cone shaped and made from Nile clay with a shelf dividing the fire below from the bread above. Most importantly, they discovered leavening, probably by accident. Some dough may have been overlooked, fermented overnight by natural air-borne yeasts, baked next day to avoid loss, and thus the first raised bread was baked. Fermentation of cereals, of course, has also been developed for the production of alcoholic beverages but this aspect of cereal products is not within the remit of this paper.

The Romans took over where the Egyptians had left off and developed the fermentation process by perfecting a bakers' balm from millet or wheat bran using the mould from wine tubs, essentially the same process as used in this country until recently. Today a strain of yeast, Bakers' yeast, *Saccharomyces cerevisiae*, is used in compressed or dried forms.

It was the Romans who invented the first rotary mill, the quern, then later an hour-glass stone over a stationary one driven by hand or animal power. Later two flat round stones, the bottom one stationary, were developed for milling and water power was applied. From Roman and Greek times flour was used straight from the mill but also as white flour after sieving. Water-mills were introduced by the Romans to Britain and the Domesday Book mentions some 5000 mills in Southern England. Windmills came in the middle ages, around 1190 AD, and at one time there were as many as 10 000 windmills in England.

However, the big advance in milling did not come until the latter part of the 19th century, when the use of horizontal steel rolls was introduced in Hungary. The first mill in Britain to use rolls was in Liverpoool in 1868 and by the 1880s rolls had largely replaced stones in most mills. Roller milling brought about a widespread change in character of the loaf as white flour became cheaper, whiter and more plentiful (and introduced greater precision and capacity). Without the use of roller milling, together with steam engines and other power sources, millers would have had great difficulty in producing sufficient flour for the needs of the rapidly increasing population of Victorian times and the urbanisation resulting from the industrial revolution.

The supply of wheat in the UK also changed dramatically in the 19th century. The Corn Laws had heavily penalised the importation of wheat but the repeal of the laws in the early part of the century, a controversial and often emotive issue, allowed access of wheat from the Continent, particularly Hungary and France and also Egypt. Later the opening up of the New World territories, particularly the North American prairies following the Civil War, and also Australia and Argentina, coupled with improved transport resulted in very cheap and excellent breadmaking quality wheats becoming available which Britain, with its economic strength, could afford to purchase.

The ready availability of white flour from this wheat allowed baking for the whole population of bold, well-risen loaves of fine, even texture and good keeping quality. This is the main type of bread the country has become used to over a period of 100 years and has been mirrored in countries of British influence which had access to good wheats such as the USA, Canada, Australia and South Africa.

Similar changes did not take place at that time on the Continent. France had always been a wheat exporting country and continued to use its soft milling, breadmaking quality wheat to make the hard crusted, open-textured baguette-type of bread while Germany clung to its rye and rye-wheat bread tradition. It is easy to see why Britain became a slicing, toasting, spreading and sandwich bread-eating nation and why the Continental countries stayed breakers of rolls eaten with meals but without butter or similar spreads.

The insistence on white bread has a long and well-documented history. White flour in earlier times was produced with difficulty by sieving. Apart from the intrinsic quality of white bread, it was expensive and could only be afforded by the rich giving rise to a bread snobbery, noted in early Greek times. In Britain, up to the middle ages, most people had to be content with a solid squat loaf made mainly from wheat but including barley, oats, rye, beans, peas and even chestnuts and acorns. As the peasant classes became freer and more affluent so the demand for white wheaten bread increased.

BAKING

Up to the 1960s all bread in this country was made by the traditional bulk fermentation method. Flour, water, yeast and salt, perhaps a little fat, were mixed into a dough and the dough developed by fermenting for at least 3 hours. During this time the yeast ferments, giving off gas which raises the dough but this is expelled later by 'knocking back'. The main object during fermentation is to develop the visco-elastic strength of the gluten by changing the structure of the proteins of the flour to give a dough that will retain gas produced at the later proving stage. Following dividing and moulding the dough is proved (i.e. further fermentation, at about 38-48°C, with the fine bubbles of CO_2 being trapped by the gluten matrix) then baked and cooled.

Around the turn of the '50s a 'no-time' batch method of dough development was introduced in the UK and became known as the Chorleywood Bread Process. The process uses high energy, high speed mixing imparting 11Wh of work/kg of dough over a 3 minute period in the presence of oxidants, usually a synergistic mixture of potassium bromate and ascorbic acid. The developed dough is then moulded, proved and baked as in the traditional long fermentation method.

The savings of time, space, skill and labour using this method were appreciable and the plant baking industry of the country rapidly changed over to the Chorleywood Bread Process in the '60s. An unpredicted benefit of the method was that flours with one percentage point less protein (i.e. 11% instead of 12%) could be used to give excellent bread indistinguishable from that made from the higher protein flours. This advantage has had enormous repercussions in the extended use of homegrown wheats, which tend to have low protein levels, to replace imported high protein North American wheat.

A further 'no-time' dough technique was the Activated Dough Development method which uses slow speed mixers in the presence of both oxidant and a reductant, cysteine. While this tends to save on time, space and labour, it does not enjoy the advantage of being able to use lower protein flours but is suitable for the smaller baker or in-store bakery.

In response to these faster methods the bulk fermentation method has in the last few years been speeded up by most craft bakers. Initial fermentation is now usually much less than one hour but a higher level of bread improvers has to be used than in the more traditional longer method.

FLOUR

Flour is produced, of course, for a variety of cereal products other than bread (Figure 1). Just short of 5m tonnes of wheat is milled each year and the bulk (some 66%) is used for breadmaking. Biscuit making takes 13.7%, household use about 5% and cake making about 2%. The remaining flours are used for a variety of purposes, such as in soups, alcoholic fermentation, gluten production, extrusion products, pasta and some non-nutritive uses. Wheats from different sources are mixed (gristed) before milling to produce flours with the required end-product specifications.

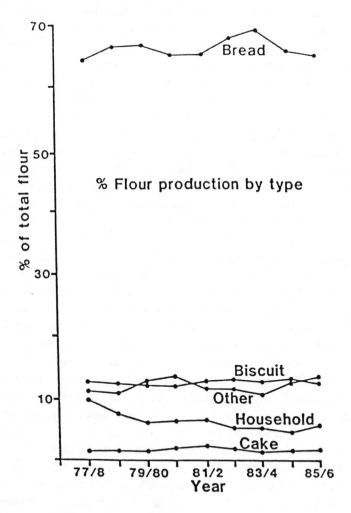

Figure 5.1   Flour use in the UK

VARIETIES OF BAKED GOODS

Biscuit flours are milled from soft milling, low protein wheats which are abundant in the UK. Breadmaking flours were traditionally milled from small amounts of UK hard milling but low protein weak wheat gristed with larger amounts of hard milling, high protein, strong North American wheats, plus some carrier intermediate protein wheats of, say Australian or Argentine origin. Hard milling wheats are preferred to give good extraction of free-running white flour, with adequate starch damage which controls water absorption in the dough. The baking strength of the North American wheat was required to produce the full-bodied, fine textured loaves to which the country had become accustomed.

Remarkable changes in the gristing pattern have occurred since the Chorleywood Bread Process was introduced (Figure 2). The method allowed more low protein, home-grown wheat to be used and firstly the carrier wheats disappeared from the grist and then the amount of North American wheat in the grist was reduced. Later, UK membership of the EEC imposed a graded introduction of a swingeing levy (now approximately £130/tonne) on importation of third country wheats and the economic incentive thus provided stimulated a further drop in the percentage of North American wheat in grist. A shortfall in availability of suitable UK wheats was made up by importation of wheat from other EEC countries, mainly France, but as the yield and total production of UK wheat rose then EEC imports dropped to negligible amounts. EEC imports now only occur in any amount when the UK has a wet harvest period and cereal alpha-amylase levels are high (e.g. in 1985/86).

Use of low protein UK wheat has been further facilitated by two technological changes. One is the addition of extra protein as gluten prepared from flour by separation from the starch; the other is the use fungal alpha-amylase. The addition of high amounts of this enzyme, another Chorleywood inspired development, allows dough expansion to continue for longer in the oven and enables loaves of appropriate quality to be baked from lower protein flours. Both these methods have been widely adopted and gluten usage in the UK in 1984-5 was 28 000 tonnes, about half of which was produced in the UK and so extended the utilization of home-grown wheat. Much of the recent increase in gluten

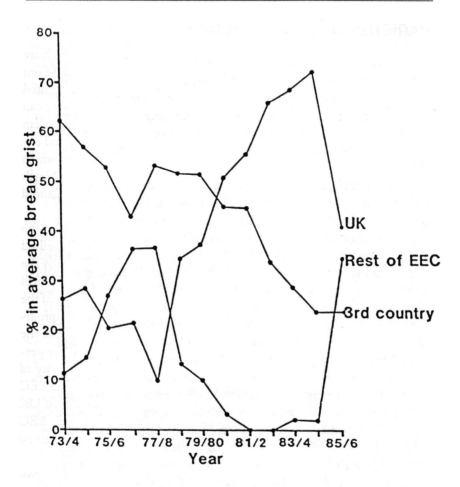

Figure 5.2   Average grist composition of UK bread

usage has been associated with the increase in consumption of high-extraction bread, brown and wholemeal.

NUTRITION

Bread is classified under the Bread and Flour Regulations into four main groups according to the flour from which it is baked. Wholemeal bread is made from flour containing the whole of the wheat, i.e. bran, germ and endosperm. Brown bread is made using brown flour containing 0.6% crude fibre, in practice about 85% extraction, and includes as much endosperm as possible, some bran, and some germ. White bread is made from flour other than brown or wholemeal flour and in practice the miller tries to scrape off the endosperm with as little contamination from bran or germ as possible. Germ bread (such as the original Hovis or Vitbe) usually has a white flour base to which 10% of heat-treated germ must be added.

In terms of major nutrients there is little to choose between the breads. They have good protein levels, adequate starch and are low in fat. White flour has still legally to have calcium, iron, thiamin and nicotinic acid added, i.e. those nutrients where bread makes a significant contribution to the nation's consumption. The higher extraction breads have higher mineral and vitamin contents (except for calcium) but taking the white bread fortification into account little effect would be seen if there was a complete switch from white to wholemeal or vice-versa as far as the main nutrients and those minerals and vitamins where bread makes a significant contribution to the total diet are concerned. Where there is a significant difference is in dietary fibre. Here bread and cereal products make a large contribution to the nation's diet but wholemeal, with its high bran content, which has an excellent faecal bulking property, contains more dietary fibre than white bread. The absolute figures vary, depending on the analytical method used but, since no one knows what the requirement for dietary fibre should be, or which particular component of the dietary fibre complex should be most promoted, perhaps it does not matter too much. However, it would be generally accepted that the ratio of dietary fibre in white, brown and wholemeal is approximately 1:2:3.

Resistant starch, formed during baking, reaches the lower bowel where it has physiological activity, and should be included in overall dietary fibre figures. In addition, with many people some natural starch, depending on its source, can reach the lower bowel in variable amount, and there increases bacterial growth and thus faecal bulk. The dangers of attempting to be too definitive about dietary fibre data based on chemical analysis of some specific groups of polysaccharides are thus evident.

As in all western countries, bread consumption in the UK has declined since Victorian times. The reasons are complex but relate to social change, politics, greater affluence, general decrease in manual work and energy needs, improved transportation of foodstuffs, improved preservation techniques and the availability of a plethora of other types of food.

It should be emphasised that the figures in Figure 3 are from the National Food Survey which measures only food consumed in the home. This has somewhat exaggerated the decline in bread consumption. Working from figures for bread wheat milled, it has been possible to show a greatly increased consumption of bread outside the home, as bar snacks, hamburger rolls, increased industrial and business catering, etc. The level of this consumption now appears to have levelled off at about 25% of total bread as reported by the National Food Survey, i.e. about one-fifth of all bread.

One thing that stands out is that the UK, like France, USA, etc., is a white bread eating nation. Until a few years ago, wholemeal bread represented only about 2% of the total and brown and germ breads about 6 or 7%. This pattern changed in the middle '70s as the dietary fibre hypothesis caught the imagination of the consumer and as wholemeal was perceived to be more 'natural' than 'refined' white. This movement resulted in increases in firstly brown then wholemeal, both at the expense of white bread (Figure 3).

The rapid increase in consumption of wholemeal bread has been greatly helped by the extension of the use of ascorbic acid as bread improver for wholemeal bread in the Bread and Flour Regulation 1983, and possibly widely anticipated in practice by a couple of years. Without ascorbic acid a wholemeal loaf tends to be dull, squat, heavy and rather tough to eat, and while, perhaps, to the taste of some on all occasions, or to all on some occasions, this was only to the extent of less than 2% of total bread. With ascorbic acid loaf volume is increased, texture is light, the bread lasts a good length of time and the loaf is more generally appealing. As a result consumption has increased to about 15% or more of all bread.

Incorporation of bran into flour, which occurs in brown and wholemeal flours, tends to reduce loaf volume and strong breadmaking wheat, particularly high-protein Canadian wheat, is still required, even with the use of ascorbic acid, to make an acceptable wholemeal loaf. With the swingeing levy on imported third country wheat the UK millers and

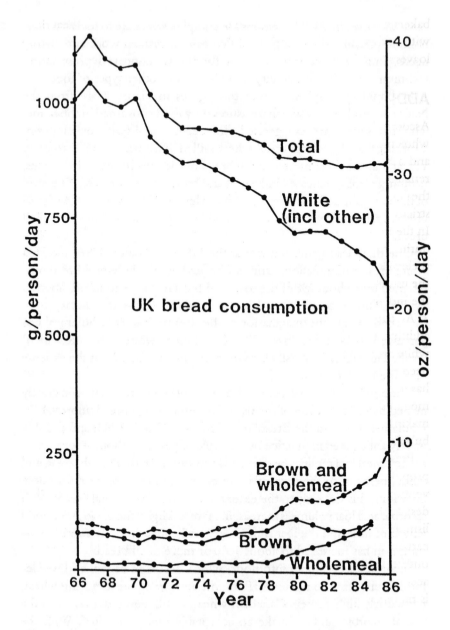

Figure 5.3   Bread consumption in the UK by bread type

bakers have turned increasingly to using more home-grown wheat flour with added gluten to improve volume and texture of high extraction loaves so as to keep the costs of the popular loaves within reasonable limits.

ADDITIVES

Ascorbic acid, used for making white bread as well as brown and wholemeal, is an 'acceptable' additive. It has the cachet of being 'natural' and a well-known vitamin, although after baking no vitamin activity remains. Other oxidising improvers used in breadmaking, particularly in the 'no time dough' processes, but also in traditional fermentation, are strictly legally controlled and have been extensively toxicologically tested. In the case of bromate, for example, it is known that it is totally changed during baking to bromide which is innocuous at the levels used. Nevertheless, labelling regulations and the increasing awareness of the public of the use of additives, and the sensitivity of major retailers, have stimulated the industry to reconsider its use of particular additives.

As consumers developed a taste for higher extraction breads and as additive awareness increased, the desirability for sparkling whiteness of white bread, which had always been seen as major customer attraction, has been re-examined. As a result the use of benzoyl peroxide to bleach flour has been largely discontinued. However, there are still a few innocuous methods the baker can use to make bread look whiter, for example by making 'four-piece bread' which results in an orientation of the gas bubbles so as to give a crumb texture which reflect more light.

Preservatives, in some strange way, have become a term of abuse, and propionate, permitted under the Bread and Flour Regulations for the prevention of rope (*B. subtilis*) in bread, is now omitted by many bakers. This despite the fact that propionate is an everyday product in human metabolism and is appreciated by gourmets as the flavour-giving substance of certain Swiss cheeses such as Emmenthal and Simmenthal. However, outbreaks of rope cannot be tolerated and propionate is often replaced by acetic acid which is not as effective as propionate but 'vinegar' on the label is more acceptable than 'preservative E.202'.

CHANGES IN THE BREAD INDUSTRY

After the end of the First World War there were some 600 millers producing flour and in 1935 there were some 24 000 bakers. Bread was largely sold by bread roundsmen or directly from the bakery/shop and perhaps even the muffin man still called.

Rationalisation has occurred for all the usual reasons, improved machinery, greater economy of scale, increasing labour costs, improved transport and distribution etc, and was considerably speeded-up by the advent of Mr Garfield Weston, a Canadian, into this country. An eminently successful baker, who took over a number of bakeries, he started to buy flour mills in the UK to ensure adequate and cheap flour supplies for his bakeries. UK millers responded by rationalising amongst themselves and protecting their outlets by buying up bakeries. Bakers became millers and millers became bakers. When the flour dust had settled, the UK was left with about 39 millers and about 89 mills plus a couple of handfuls of small stone-millers whose contribution to overall flour milled is negligible. Of the roller millers, three companies account for some 80% of all flour milled.

In the baking trade, the independent master bakers or craft bakers who worked largely by hand were badly affected by the growth of plant-baking of bread involving flow-line production, mechanical slicing and wrapping and wholesale retailing. Of recent times, the development of the 'hot bread' shops and in-store bakeries by the supermarket chains (about 560 in 1984), based on the smell and attractive appearance of freshly baked well-crusted loaves, made by semi-skilled workers, has affected the master baker yet again. Probably only about 4000 craft bakers still exist but they still account for some 26% of bread output by volume. In-store bakeries probably now account for 4% but this sector is growing.

Plant bakeries, however, predominate, accounting for about 70% of all bread. Two companies (who are also two of the three main milling companies) account for 59% of all bread by volume, and about 90% of wrapped and sliced bread either branded or own label. The other 20 plant bakeries account for the remaining 11% of total bread sold.

In terms of bread processes used, the Chorleywood Bread Process accounts for about 75-80% of all bread sold, including morning goods and the Activated Dough Development method accounts for another 10%; the two no time dough processes clearly being suited to the in-store bakeries and hot-bread shops as well as to the plant baker. Traditional bulk fermentation, in its modern rapid form, is limited to craft bakers and a few plant bakeries.

VARIETY BREADS

On entering the average supermarket it is striking to see the very wide range of bread products now on sale. Not only white, brown, wholemeal, sliced/unsliced, heavily/lightly crusted, wrapped, unwrapped and permutations thereof, but all variations in size and shape, with incorporation of pea fibre, malted grains, softened grains, dusted with seeds of various kinds as well as stoneground and ethnic breads. Bread no longer seems to be price sensitive, yet only a few years ago the price of bread was strictly controlled. Greater consumer awareness and greater affluence has encouraged the supermarkets, particularly, to stack their shelves to tempt their customers. A few years ago such goods would have remained unsold.

A further illustration of this movement is the buoyancy (increase of 25% in value from 1983-85) of 'morning goods', a trade name covering rolls, baps, scones, crumpets, croissants and related items. These are in demand for a variety of meal occasions, as treats, and for the impulse purchaser. In financial terms morning goods are about 36% of the value of the bread market.

OTHER CEREAL PRODUCTS

The UK has the highest *per capita* consumption of biscuits and, while consumption in the home is only of the order of 5oz/person/week (compared with bread at 30oz/week), the value of the biscuit market is about 60% of the bread market, two companies having over 60% of the business. Consumption was generally steady after a small fall in the mid-70s (5.35oz/person/week in 1975, 5.09 in 1984) but started to rise again in 1985 and in 1986 was 5.42oz/person/week. Chocolate biscuits, which show positive price elasticity, have increased as a greater proportion of the total, reflecting greater affluence, and high-fibre, additive free, 'healthy' biscuits and crispbreads are growing in popularity.

Both biscuits and cakes have relatively high fat and sugar contents and have suffered from the increased health awareness as well as from social changes. For example, afternoon tea as an English institution has greatly declined. Cakes have suffered more than biscuits and consumption (in the home) fell from 5.19oz in 1970 to 3.5oz in 1984, with the packaged cake market being largely static, but coming under pressure from fresh cakes, from in-store bakeries and from frozen cakes.

Breakfast cereal consumption, on the other hand, has increased (1.8oz/ person/week in 1960 to 4.38 in 1986) as the traditional British cooked breakfast (including porridge) has declined and as increased health aware- ness has boosted the bran and muesli sectors. Breakfast cereal sales are about 30% the value of bread sales although in volume terms they are very much smaller. Some other cereal products, such as cereal or granola bars, are showing an equally dynamic trend. Pasta, starting from a low base, is becoming more popular; mainly the canned variety, but the dried pasta market is growing by about 10% each year by volume. 'Healthier' eating is even being reflected in traditional dry pasta products, and wholemeal pasta now constitutes about 15% of the total dried pasta market. Rice too, like pasta, is becoming more accepted as a potato substitute probably helped by ethnic influences. Traditional products and new cereal snack products are being made, using high temperature, short time, extrusion.

Home baking has been in decline for some years as reflected in decreased sales of household flour and cake mixes.

CONCLUSION

In summary, the use of cereals in human nutrition has a long and ancient tradition and many of the products we eat today are little different from those eaten 2000 years ago. While bread consumption has been in decline for most of this century the 'naturalness' of cereals, their high starch and fibre content and the low fat content of bread should, in the light of present nutritional dogma, all tend to reverse the decline, aided by the ingenuity of bakers in catering to perceived values.

Other bakery products are being changed and lower fat and sugar and higher fibre recipes are being evolved. Traditional products are being promoted on 'a little of what you fancy does you good' basis; a luxury to be enjoyed; cut down on something else for a change if you must. Other cereal products, particularly breakfast cereals, pasta, and rice, while still only a small proportion of total cereals eaten, should continue to show growth.

6
Sugars and sugar processing
R. C. RIGHELATO

For most of mankind the prime sources of food energy are the storage products of plants: carbohydrates and triglycerides. The most ubiquitous stores are the carbohydrates which are found in the seeds, stems and roots of a wide range of plants. In them glucose and fructose are stored largely as polymers, starches and fructans, or as oligomers, predominantly sucrose (Table 1). Whilst the crops themselves are seasonal, processing techniques developed in antiquity, often involving dehydration or fermentation, enabling the food to be stablilised and made available all year round. Fruits and vegetables were dried; the juice from the stem of sweet grasses was evaporated to make a solid sugar product; juices of many fruits were fermented, so preserving most of the energy value of the sugars as alcohol. Today's food industry has developed from this craft base, over the last few centuries, to feed much larger numbers of people living largely in urban

Table 6.1 Carbohydrate crops

Starch crops	Wheat, maize, barley, rice, cassava, potato
Sugar crops	Cane, sweet sorghum, beetroot, carrot, sugar beet
Fructans	Jerusalem artichoke, chickory

101

environments. In doing so in the UK we have developed the ability to produce, store and deliver several hundred million tonnes of food commodities and to provide an increasing variety of safe, nutritious and interesting prepared foods. Here I chronicle the history of the provision of sugars as key food ingredients, then examine their role in what we eat today and lastly look at what changes we can expect as we approach AD 2000.

SUGAR PRODUCTION

The 'sweet grass' from which today's sugar cane was derived was used in the Indian subcontinent at least three thousand years ago. Known as the 'Persian reed' it was brought to Europe in the seventh century AD by the prophet Mohammed during the Islamic wars.

Primitive milling technology existed in the Middle Ages in several places around the Mediterranean. However, it was only with the colonisation of the West Indies and the development of an industrial processing technology in the eighteenth century that sugar became available in any quantity in Europe. The crop and processing methods have become more efficient but are in essence the same today as in 1800. Sugar cane is a large bamboo-like grass which accumulates sucrose in the pith cells of the stem. It is one of the most efficient converters of solar energy into carbohydrates, producing up to 50 tonnes dry biomass per hectare, half of which is sucrose. The cane is usually cut annually for two to six years, then new lengths of stem planted as new stock. Cut cane is soon spoilt by bacterial growth on the sugary sap, so it has to be quickly processed. It is chopped into short lengths and crushed in large mills, separating the juice from the fibre, 'bagasse', which is burnt to provide the energy used in the process.

To the juice, which contains 11–14% sucrose, lime is added and carbon dioxide bubbled through. The calcium carbonate precipitate so formed is floated off as a scum, removing with it soil debris, cell debris and other contaminating material. The clarified juice is then concentrated by evaporation and the sucrose crystallised out by boiling the saturated solution under vacuum, keeping the temperature around 75°C. The 'raw sugar' crystals are centrifuged from the mother liquor or 'molasses'. Raw sugar is around 98% sucrose, 1.0% other sugars and 1.0% inorganics. It is mostly in this form that sugar is transported in bulk around the world. To make white sugar, the raw sugar is dissolved in water and undergoes a repeat of the processes of clarification and crystallisation. This secondary refining is usually done in the country of final use. As well as white sugar and molasses, the sugar processors provide a range of products containing varying amounts of the flavour, colour and other components of the cane molasses. These range from the heavy, dark muscovado sugars which are about 20% molasses, to the washed raws and 'golden granulated' which are over 99% sucrose.

Sugar cane was virtually the sole source of sugar until the middle of the nineteenth century when beet was developed in Europe, spurred on by the blockade of the continental ports by the Royal Navy in the Napoleonic wars. In temperate countries the swollen tap roots of plants such as carrots, beetroot or turnip contain sucrose as the storage carbohydrate. A species of beet, *Beta vulgaris*, was developed for sucrose production in temperate regions unsuitable for sugar cane. The process is essentially similar to that of cane sugar production, though it is more energy-intensive as there is no bagasse to provide fuel. There is, however, a beet pulp, left after extracting the juice, which is an important by-product used for feeding cattle and which is being developed as a human dietary fibre product. The white sugar from cane and beet are to all intents and purposes identical. However, the brown sugars generally use the pleasant flavours of raw cane sugar or cane molasses.

In Europe now 90% of our sugar comes from sugar beet; a residual 1.3 million tonnes of cane sugar is imported from many African, Caribbean and Pacific countries under the Lomé convention. Because of its Commonwealth associations most of the cane sugar comes to the United Kingdom. Annual consumption of 2.2 million tonnes of sucrose is supplied half by home grown beet and half from cane sugar imported from the Third World. Price and volume of production is controlled by the Common Agricultural Policy. Quotas are set to ensure an adequate supply of sugar, resulting in surpluses in most years. Price is set to give the farmers a reasonable return, and is normally well above the so-called World price which in fact represents a relatively small market of less than 20% of total world sugar production.

Sugars can also be produced from starches by enzymic hydrolysis and isomerisation (Dziedzic and Kearsley, 1984). In some countries which have high support prices for sucrose, notably the USA, these products now form half of the total market for sugar and sugar syrups. In the European Community, however, the production of fructose syrups is restricted by quota to a relatively small quantity, though glucose is unrestricted and competes freely with sucrose in some uses. The other significant source of simple sugars is milk; whey powders and lactose are used widely in foods, though the total amount consumed is small compared with sucrose and the starch syrups. Ignoring lactose, the contribution of sugars from cane, beet and cereals to the UK food supply is 2.6 million tonnes per year, 2.2 million as sucrose and 0.4 million as starch derived sugars.

SUGARS CONSUMPTION PATTERNS

The main role of dietary carbohydrate is the provision of energy; sucrose, the dominant simple sugar used in making foods, probably accounts for 10%-20% of our energy needs. Current average supply in the UK is approximately 104g per person per day (MAFF, 1984). Actual consumption is lower owing to wastage which could be between 10 and 30% (Glinsman *et al.*, 1986) and use of part of the sugar supply for fermentation. Whilst the UK consumption of all sugars has fallen from a peak of around 145g/day in 1960 to approximately 124g today, as a proportion of total food energy it has changed little over at least the last fifty years (BNF 1987).

During this period there have been substantial changes in the sorts of food that are eaten and in their place of manufacture. Increasingly we have been buying more prepared and part-prepared foods, and an increasing variety of foods, rather than individual commodities, for home cooking. This is clearly reflected in the sugar consumption statistics. Purchases of sugar into the home have fallen steadily and industrial consumption has increased by a roughly equivalent amount (Figure 1).

Sugars are rarely consumed on their own; they are usually part of a food product, added to give flavour, structure and for a variety of other functions. The main foods in which sugars feature are those containing cereals and fruit and in confectionery and soft drinks (Table 2). In smaller

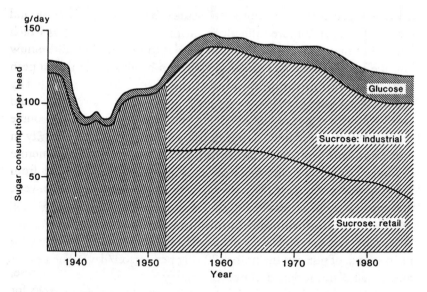

Figure 6.1   Changes in sugars consumption in the UK.

Table 6.2   Sugars consumed in prepared foods

	g/day	%
Baked goods	10.3	19
Cereals	3.2	6
Fruit and preserves	8.2	15
Confectionery	8.7	16
Chocolate	11.9	22
Soft drinks	6.3	12
Others	5.4	10

(Source: MAFF, 1984. Natural Food Survey and Trade Estimates, assumes 10% wastage)

amounts sugars are used to improve the taste of a wide variety of sweet and savoury foods. It is more difficult to quantify the uses of sugars in the home, but they appear to be broadly similar to prepared foods brought into the home; sweetening tea and coffee, on breakfast cereals and fruit, in baking and in preparing sauces.

There has been a growth over the last few years in the use of a widening range of brown sugars and the so-called 'unrefined' sugars, which are raw sugars subject to additional purification steps to make them fit for consumption. These sugars contribute pleasant flavours and small amounts of mineral micronutrients, more or less in proportion to their colour or the proportion of molasses that they contain. In dietary terms the micronutrient contribution could only be significant for the very dark soft browns and muscovado sugars (Table 3); those sugars could provide 10-20% of the recommended daily intake of iron and calcium if they were the main source of sugar in the home (20-40g per person/day). Their prime nutritional contribution is, however, energy.

For most people in the UK simple sugars contribute between 10% and 20% of energy needs. Most of the sugars and other carbohydrates have a caloric value of 3.75 kcal/g, though a few may be poorly metabolised and may be used in reduced calorie foods. There have been a number of recent

Table 6.3   Mineral contents of sugars

Sugar	Fe	Ca mg/100g	Zn
Raw	1.1	24	0.05
White	0.02	0.95	0.001
Light soft brown	0.45	35	0.02
Dark soft brown	1.9	96	0.07
Muscovado	3.0	180	0.20
RDI (mg/day)	10	500	15

reviews on the nutrition and physiology of sugar (Glinsman *et al.*, 1986) to which the reader is referred for scientific reviews of sugars and health.

THE FUNCTIONALITIES OF SUGARS

Few foods, however, are used simply for nutrition; to be eaten, a food product has also to be safe and attractive; hence their ingredients must have a range of other properties, or functionalities, which are equally important. The key functionalities of sugars hinge around their crystalline nature, their interactions with water, their taste and sweetness.

Sucrose readily forms an anhydrous orthorhombic crystal from a saturated solution. The sucrose crystal, unlike the crystals of most other sugars, has a low affinity for water and so remains dry and free-flowing up to very high relative humidities. Because of this it can be cheaply transported and stored and, in the home, kept in bags and bowls without becoming sticky and caking. This is a key feature in the use of micro-crystalline and milled sugars as dispersing aids in dry mix products, in dustings and similar uses. The crystalline structure is also important in making chocolate; the continuous fat phase is filled with small sugar crystals. The proportion and size of the sugar crystals determine the texture and snap.

Most of the functionality of sugars in making foods are a consequence of their interactions with water and hydrophilic polymers. All polyols interact with water. Though the relationship between structure and activity is poorly understood, it is presumed to be a function of the steric availability of hydroxyl groups and their potentiality for hydrogen-bonding to water, or substituting for water in interactions with biopolymers. Empirically it is found that the more soluble sugars are generally most useful. For example, the gelatinisation temperature for wheat starch can be raised from around 60°C in water to 100°C in the presence of 2.5M sucrose (Jacobsburg and Daniels, 1984). In making biscuits the sugar dissolves, holding the water as the biscuit heats up, so retarding the hydration of starch (Abboud and Hoseney, 1984). Water is driven off during baking, leaving a supersaturated sucrose solution from which the sugar recrystallises. The crystallinity combined with the relatively poorly hydrated starch gives the short, crisp texture to the biscuit.

Differential scanning calorimetry shows clearly the effect of sucrose in increasing the temperature at which starch gelatinises and egg white coagulates (Donovan, 1977; Donovan *et al.*, 1975). In baking cakes this temperature is raised to about 100°C for both polymers; the swelling of the starch granules and the denaturing of the ovalbumin occurs simultaneously, fixing the foamed structure.

Another type of hydrophilic interaction is that of sucrose on water activity and hence on product safety. Water activity is measured as the water vapour pressure over a solution, relative to the vapour pressure of pure water. Few microbes can grow at water activities of less than 0.8 which are generated by sucrose solutions of around 65% w/w. This effect is the basis of preservation of fruits as jams, and a contribution to the storage life of cakes, creams, etc. The high affinity of sugars for water and for hydrophilic polymers such as starches has important effects on the staling of cakes, the texture of icings and fondants and many other foods.

Although sugars are generally chemically stable in cooking, trace amounts can react with other components to contribute to the taste and appearance of foods. Sucrose being a non-reducing sugar, is relatively unreactive. The reducing sugars (glucose and more particularly fructose) take part in Maillard reactions, giving reaction products which impart flavour and brown colours (Hurell, 1982). Unreacted, sugars enhance and modify many other tastes and flavours, both sweet and savoury.

The craft of cooking evolved using all of these, and other, properties of sugars to make the products with which we are familiar. As more of the cooking is done by food manufacturers the technological description of the craft has grown, though still poorly backed by scientific understanding of the physics and chemistry behind the technology.

The main organoleptic property of sugar is, of course, sweetness. We are born with a liking for sweet things (Birch, 1987) and the idea of sweetness extends by metaphor from food into many other aspects of life. The evolutionary significance of sweetness lies presumably in its association with safe sources of dietary energy and a liking for sweet-tasting foods is widely found amongst mammals. Whilst this results in a preference for sugars, the response to other sweeteners varies within and between species, indicating differences in the detail of sweetness perception. Taste receptors are less well understood than some other cell receptors, however, it appears that a sweetener has to fit into a slot in the receptor; binding requires a hydrophobic region and a polar region, and that excitation requires reciprocal hydrogen bonding through two sites 2.8–3.0 Angstrom apart (Birch, 1987). Interestingly, within a homologous series of structures, increasing lipophilicity increases sweetness up to a maximum beyond which the compounds are perceived as bitter, suggesting a relationship between the receptors for sweetness and for bitterness. It is currently thought that sweeteners form a reversible complex with the receptor which causes a permeability change in the receptor cell membranes, triggering the release of the synaptic vesicles containing a neurotransmitter (Brand, 1978).

The link between the sensory properties of foods, and their assimilation, and appetite control is an important, but poorly understood area. Intense sweeteners and sugars provide a means of separating the sensory response from the caloric response to a food and are the subject of much current research (Porikos and van Itallie, 1984). The effect of sweetness *per se* on satiety is not entirely clear. Whatever its short-term effects, it appears that mechanisms may exist through which we control our calorie intake that override the taste-related influences on eating. Reports on the substitution of sugars with intense sweeteners show subjects sometimes compensating for 'lost' calories by eating more of other foods (Rolls, 1987) and that use of sugar substitutes does not itself bring about weight reduction (BNF, 1987; Drewnowski *et al.*, 1985).

The relationship between preference for fatty foods and for sweet foods is of interest as fats and carbohydrates constitute the majority of our dietary energy. There appears to be a negative correlation between liking for sweet foods and liking of fat foods (Grinker, 1978; Nelson, 1985). In recent studies of individual's food consumption in the UK (Nelson, 1985) and Eire (Gibney *et al.*, 1987), high sugar consumers tended to have a low fat consumption and *vice versa*. In the UK study those who achieved a fat consumption equal to the recommended 35% of energy consumed 25% of their energy as total sugars. In the Eire study, the low fat group (33% of energy) consumed 19.1% energy from sugar; the high fat group (49.1% of energy) consumed 12.6% of energy from sugar. This inverse relationship between sugars and fats consumption accords with the experimental preference data (Nelson, 1985), and with the distribution of fats and sugars in the food supply. 70% of fats are consumed in essentially sugar-free products and 70% of sugars are consumed in low fat (less than 30% of energy as fat) products.

SUGAR SUBSTITUTES

In recent years a range of products designed as alternatives to sugars, other carbohydrates and fats have appeared. The objective is usually to provide a lower calorie product. The consumer demand for low-calorie products has been amply demonstrated by the rapid growth of the diet soft drink market in the USA. In soft drinks sugars are used only for their sweetness. Once an adequate quality low calorie sweetener was available the market expanded by over 15%, with little or no change in the consumption of the regular caloric drinks. It is now technically possible to produce many alternative soft drinks, without significantly compromising sensory quality, because a wide range of higher quality sweeteners is becoming available. About one third of sugar consumption is used in sweetening soft drinks and hot beverages. For those needing to reduce their energy consumption or wishing to take sweet drinks without adding calories, these uses are entirely substitutable by very low calorie diet products.

It is technically much more difficult to provide the other properties of sugars in a low calorie form. These largely depend on the hydrophilic nature of sugars and they cannot be provided by trace quantities of high intensity sweeteners. Their substitution with an unmetabolised bulk material presents a physiological dilemma. Hydrophilic low molecular weight products which are not absorbed can cause osmotic diarrhoea. Absorption, were it to occur and the component not be metabolised, would probably present problems of subsequent elimination. In practice, most of the reduced calorie ingredients are to some extent metabolised by the microflora of the large intestine. Excessive fermentation can cause intestinal discomfort as well as converting the ingredient in part to fatty acids which are assimilated and contribute dietary energy.

There are no low calorie products available in the UK that provide all of the functions of sucrose and glucose. A number of approved ingredients can be used, which give a partial calorie reduction, though sometimes it is necessary to use them with preservatives and other additives to produce safe and acceptable products. These include some of the sugar alcohols, some cellulose products, polydextrose and a range of dietary fibre products from natural sources. As well as reduced-calorie ingredients, there is a range of speciality carbohydrates developed by the sugar industry and the starch industry. These are mostly enzymically produced sugars with particular functionalities required for special applications. For example, isomaltulose and neo-sugar made from sucrose are used in Japan as non-cariogenic sugars in confectionery.

CONCLUSIONS

Sugars are provided in a wide range of forms, crystalline and liquid, for both the domestic user and the food manufacturer. These range from pure granulated sugar to the highly flavoured syrups and treacles. Whilst small amounts of minerals are present in the darker sugars or syrups the major nutritional role of sugars is the provision of energy. As well as providing energy they are essential to the taste, structure and stability of many foods. These functional properties of sugars depend on their interaction with water and hydrophilic polymers in foods, and on their high stability.

High intensity sweeteners can be used as alternatives to sugar where sweetness is the only function provided. In most food products, however, other functions are also needed and substitution is more difficult. Nonetheless the industry is providing the choice of an increasing range of products with differing nutrition, flavour and functional features.

References

Abboud, A. M. and Hoseney, R. C. (1984) *Cereal Chem.*, 61, 34-7

Birch, G. G. (1987) In Dobbing, J. (ed.) *Sweetness* pp. 3-13 (Springer Verlag, London)

BNF (1987). *'Sugars and syrups'*. (British Nutrition Foundation, London)

Booth, D. A. (1986). *European nutrition report*, No.7

Brand, J. G. (1978). In Shaw, J. H. and Roussos, G. G. (eds.) *Sweeteners and dental caries* pp. 13-32 (Karger, Basel)

Donovan, J. W., Mapes, C. J., Davies, J. G. and Garibaldi, J. A.(1975). *J. Sci. Food Agric.*, 26, 73-83

Donovan, J. W. (1977). *J. Sci. Food Agric.*, 28, 571-8

Drewnowski, A., Brunzell, J. D., Sande, K., Ivenius, P. H. and Greenwood, H. R. C. (1985). *Physiol. Behaviour*, 35, 17–22

Dziedzic, S. Z. and Kearsley, M. W. (1984) *Glucose syrups: Science and
technology*. (Elsevier, London)

Gibney, M. J., Maloneym, M. and Shelley, E. (1978). *Proc. Nutr. Soc.*, 46,
14A

Glinsman, W. H., Irausquin, H. and Park, Y. K. (1986). Report on
evaluation of health aspects of sugars contained in carbohydrate
sweeteners. *J. Nutr.*, 11S

Grinker, J. A. (1978). *Amer. J. Clin. Nutr.*, 31, 1078–87

Hurell, R. F. (1982). In Morton, I. D. and Macleod, A. J. (eds.) *Food
Flavors* pp. 399–438 (Elsevier, Oxford)

Jacobsburg, F. R. and Daniels, N. W. R. (1984). *Chemistry and industry*,
December, 1007–8

MAFF (1984). *Household food consumption and expenditure*. (HMSO,
London)

Mizukoshi, M., Kawada, T. and Matsui, N. (1979). *Cereal Chem.*, 56,
305–9

Nelson, H. (1985). *Human Nutr. Appl. Nutr.*, 39A, 456–64

Porikos, K. P. and van Itallie, T. B. (1984). In Steginck, L. D. and Filer,
L. J. (eds.) *Aspartame physiology and biochemistry* pp. 273–86 (Decker,
New York)

Rolls, B. (1987). In Dobbing, J. (ed.) *Sweetness* pp. 161–73 (Springer
Verlag, London)

7
Meat and meat products

A. J. BAILEY

The earliest forms of meat processing must have involved preservation by cooking, drying and by the addition of salt. The Romans are believed to be the first to use ice as a preservative. Processing techniques continued to develop in order to spread the availability of meat throughout the seasons, and, as urban areas developed, to ensure preservation during transport. From these early beginnings, commercial freezing and automated methods of smoking and curing hams were developed. However, no new preservation methods were introduced until canning was developed in the 1880s. Since that time many new methods have been added, for example, chemical additives, enzyme treatment, freeze drying and irradiation.

All these methods were developed to inhibit microbial spoilage, but at the same time led to an increase in the variety of meat products available to the consumer. Today almost half the total meat produced is processed in some way or other. With the basic principles of spoilage now well understood and therefore controllable, the emphasis on processing is towards consumer convenience. The power of the consumer is having a dramatic effect on the direction and structure of the meat industry and should therefore be analysed in some detail. The pressures from the consumer can be listed as follows:

- Change in shopping habits.
- Change in age profiles of consumers, and hence their needs.
- Change to convenience foods.
- Change to an expectation of variety and new products.
- Change in health awareness.
- Change to 'natural foods'.
- Change in awareness of animal welfare issues.
- Change in the meat species consumed (See Figure 1).

These changes have led to a dramatic increase in the demand for lean meat. In fact, the cost of putting on fat compared to lean is high in terms of feed costs hence the change is financially beneficial to the industry. The pig industry has responded well in reducing the fat level of pig meat over the past few years. The beef industry is now using leaner animals but the increase in lean/fat ratio has been less dramatic. The sheep industry has barely responded despite the clear indication from the consumer that fat lamb is rejected with a consequent fall in consumption. Other changes are

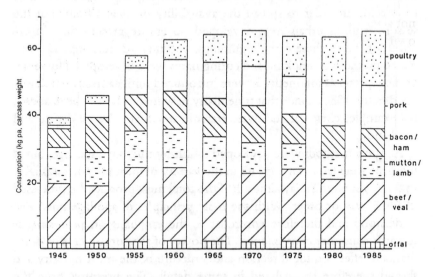

Figure 7.1   Trends in UK per capita meat consumption, 1945 to 1986.
(Source: MAFF and MLC)

the preference for 'fresh' rather than frozen and for portion control instead of large family joints. Although fresh meat sales still command 55% of the market, there is a steadily increasing change to processed meats. Some interaction between the different trends can be discerned. For example, the rapidly growing convenience food sector is thought to have particular market potential for low-calorie dishes. Many ready meals are aimed at the higher quality market compared to, say, fish fingers.

A major effect of these is that large multiple retailers have acquired a powerful position in the industry, so much so that there is now a complete reversal in the control of an industry originally dominated by the producer. That is, the consumer influences the retailer who then pressurises the processor, who in turn pressurises the slaughterhouse. Hence the producer is being forced to provide the raw material under strict specification. Producers are therefore more concerned than in the past with quality rather than quantity. The consumer and retailer are exerting an ever-increasing pressure on quality control in the industry, and this can only be for the good of the industry in the long term. The influences of consumer pressure are summarised in Figure 2.

It should be pointed out however, that pressures from the consumer are not always in the interest of the meat industry, nor even always in their own interest. For example, meat is the major source of food-borne illness,

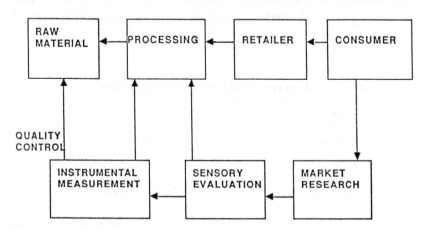

Figure 7.2   Consumer pressure

and over the years has led to numerous deaths. Despite this the consumer rates microbial contamination a low priority, placing the removal of chemical additives as their major priority (Table 1). Additives can produce allergies but they are rare, and deaths from the additives used in meat products are even rarer. However, the consumer is pressing for the removal of traditional preservatives, e.g. salts and some antioxidants, and the retailers are having to concede. Consequently there are many products currently on the shelves that have not been evaluated for shelf-life or, more importantly, for any possible changes in microbial flora. The industry must not be pressed too far since serious outbreaks could be counter-productive.

The accelerating change from fresh meat sales to processed products has not taken place uniformly across the various meat species. In the early part of the century pork was the major meat being processed, but beef is now processed to an increasing degree. However, it must be said that the poultry industry over the past 10-20 years has led the way in the use of boneless meat and other processed convenience products. Poultry's competitive price advantage has more recently been enhanced by the consumer's perception of its nutritional and quality image.

Meat has traditionally required the longest period of preparation of the foods that make up a meal, and has therefore benefitted from the development of convenience products. More recently, restructured 'steaklets' provide a better image and a convenience product for low grade

Table 7.1   Perception of food hazard priorities

Consumer	Industry
1. Food additives	1. Microbiology
2. Pesticides	2. Nutrition
3. Nutrition	3. Food additives
4. Microbiology	4. Pesticide residues

cuts. Other convenience meat items, such as pizza and ready meals, are increasing rapidly. The explosion of ready meals over the past few years illustrates the case dramatically. The market value of ready meals has been estimated to have increased by 33% in 1984-85. It is important to realise that in these convenience packages meat is still the major contributor to the meal. Marketing men are now convinced that 30 minutes preparation time appears to be the maximum for the 'active' members of society, at whom the meat trade should be aiming its products. Just as growth of frozen food sales related to home ownership of freezers, the demand for convenience foods appears to be related to the increased ownership of microwave cookers. Currently estimated at 40%, ownership is expected to increase to 80% or so by 1990.

There appears to be little doubt that the demand for convenience food will increase in the future, and this must involve more processing and cooking. In addition there is an increased demand for novelty products, together with increased eating satisfaction. The total consumption of meat is therefore being retained at a fairly steady level, although the type of meat and its extent of processing is changing dramatically. The pressure for further processing is therefore coming from the consumer, despite the counter-claims of the anti-meat lobby (a small but vociferous group) for less processing and more 'natural' food. Although growing, this will remain a small sector of the market. The demand for convenience is much greater, and this will mean an overall increase in meat processing.

COMPOSITION AND NUTRITIVE VALUE OF MEAT

The composition and nutritive value of fresh meat has been extensively studied, and meat has been recognised as a highly nutritious food, being a source of high quality protein, rich in the B vitamins, and an excellent source of essential minerals. In the average diet, meat provides 50% of our dietary proteins and 30% of our energy, and is a major source of vitamins and minerals, particularly the B vitamins and iron.

The nutritional needs of the more developed countries are met to a large extent by foods of animal origin. However, questions are now being raised as to the relationship between diet and health and disease, and the role of animal foods is highly controversial. The major objection is fat, on the basis of its high calorie content, possibly leading to obesity, and its postulated role in vascular disorders. Unfortunately 'red meat' is often included in these objections, although the fat content of lean meat is very low, i.e. less than 5%, and is visible and readily removed. Meat accounts for about 22% of fat consumed in the average diet, compared to 42% from dairy foods (Figure 3).

Nutrient variability

The most comprehensive source listing the components of meat is the update of McCance and Widdowson's 'Composition of Foods' by Paul and Southgate, 1978. The concentration of the various constituents is given in Table 2.

Figure 7.3   Proportions of fat in the average diet

Table 7.2   Composition of fresh meats

	Water	Protein	Fat	Ash
		(% by weight)		
Lean beef	65	18	5	1.0
Lean veal	75	20	6	1.0
Lean lamb	70	20	5	1.5
Lean pork	55 – 60	15 – 20	6	1.0
Pork sausage	40	10	50	—

The precise composition of meat is highly variable throughout the carcass because of the different proportion of muscle, fatty tissue, tendons, bones and edible organs. It is therefore necessary to specify the cut when discussing composition. Even the variation occurring between species, between breeds, and with the age of the animal should be taken into account.

Animal fats are glycerol esters of straight chain carboxylic acids or triglycerides. The other types of fat are the phospholipids which, although important as key components of cell membranes, are only present in small quantities, i.e. about 1% of the lean. Phospholipids are readily oxidised and therefore play an important role in the development of flavour.

Fat is a major contributor of energy or calories in the diet, and also supplies the essential fatty acids, that is linolenic and linoleic. Although meat is usually referred to as a source of 'saturated fat', in fact less than half (45%) the fat in lean cuts is saturated. Furthermore, there are distinct differences in the levels of unsaturated fat between the species, the level of unsaturation, mainly oleic acid, increases from cattle to sheep to pig meat (Table 3).

Cholesterol is a minor component of animal tissues, where it occurs free or combined with a fatty acid. Lean beef, pork and lamb contain about 70 mg cholesterol per 100 gm (compared to 250 mg in eggs). Liver

Table 7.3   Fatty acids in lean beef, pork and lamb

	Beef	Pork (% of total fat)	Lamb
Palmitic	30	28	25
Stearic	20	13	25
Oleic	40	45	40
Linoleic	2	10	5

and brain contain larger amounts, approximately 5–10 times as much.

The proteins are probably the most important constituent of meat. Muscle contains three different types of protein, the myofibrillar or salt-soluble protein, the sarcoplasmic or soluble protein, and the connective tissue or insoluble proteins. The myofibrillar proteins actin and myosin are the major (80%) proteins of muscle, acting as the contractile apparatus for locomotion in the living animal. The sarcoplasmic proteins include a wide range of oxidative and degradative enzymes, haem pigments and glyco-lytic enzymes that control many tissue functions of the living muscle. They represent about 10% of the total protein.

In contrast to the sarcoplasmic and myofibrillar proteins, the connec-tive tissue proteins collagen and elastin are low in some essential amino acids, such as, lysine, tryptophan and cysteine. However, the proportion of these proteins is too small (<5%) to affect the nutritional quality of the meat.

Carbohydrates are also present in muscle primarily as glycogen (about 1%) but most of this disappears during the development of rigor mortis and conversion to meat, meat is therefore very low in carbohydrates.

Vitamins may be classified as fat-soluble or water-soluble, the former including vitamins A, D, E or K and the latter the vitamin B complex and vitamin C. Meat is an excellent source of the B vitamins but is low in the

Table 7.4 Vitamin content of meat

Vitamin	Beef	Pork	Mutton	Liver
		(Int. units/100gm raw meat)		
A	—	—	—	20 000
B_1 Thiamin	0.07	1	0.1	0.3
B_2 Riboflavin	0.2	0.2	0.2	3
Nicotinic acid	5	5	5	13
Pantothenic acid	0.4	0.6	0.5	8
B	3	4	3	100
Folic acid	10	3	3	300
B_6	0.3	0.5	0.4	0.7
B_{12}	2	2	2	50
C	0	0	0	30
D	trace	trace	trace	45

fat-soluble vitamins (Table 4). Meat contributes substantially to the
dietary requirements of man in terms of the B complex vitamins, thiamin,
riboflavin, niacin, panthothenic acids, vitamin B_6, folic acid, biotin and
and vitamin B_{12}. Liver possesses much higher proportions of the vitamins
than skeletal muscle. Meat is an important source of vitamin B_{12} since this
vitamin is not present in plant foods.

Significant losses of these nutrients can occur via drip from the freshly
cut surface of meat, particularly newly thawed meat, and can contain an
appreciable proportion of B vitamins. Most of the vitamins are relatively
stable during cooking, but thiamin and vitamin B_6 are heat-labile and
partially destroyed by cooking, average losses being around 25%.

Meat is also an excellent source of trace elements such as zinc and iron,
and is a significant source of P, K and Na. Iron in meat is in a highly
utilisable 'haem iron' form, which is more readily absorbed than the iron

in other foods. Zinc and copper are readily chelated in high–fibre carbo-hydrate foods, whilst in meat they are in a highly bioavailable form. Meat is, however, low in calcium.

EFFECTS OF COOKING ON THE NUTRITIVE VALUE OF MEAT

In general, conventional cooking has little effect on protein and fat, but the losses in vitamins can be considerable, although it is difficult to be precise in view of the various methods of cooking, e.g. roasting, frying, broiling. The loss of thiamin, which is the most sensitive vitamin can be quite high (40-50%). Riboflavin and niacin losses are much smaller (10-20%). Loss of nutrients on cooking are, as with most other foods, substantial, but despite this meat still supplies a significant amount to the diet.

In summary the concentrations of protein and fat in average muscle varies only slightly between species but the levels of vitamins and minerals may vary considerably, e.g. high thiamin in pigmeat and high iron or zinc in beef or mutton. The most striking differences occur between the muscle and offal and indeed between the various offal tissue. Liver and kidney are excellent sources of folic acid, and liver is rich in vitamin A and vitamin D.

PRODUCTION PRACTICES

Can the nutritive value of meat be manipulated by production practices? There is little difference in the nutrient value of the different species. The only significant differences are afforded by comparison of the offal tissues. The only significant change that can be achieved by production practices is a reduction in the subcutaneous and intramuscular fat, and the possibility of increasing the proportion of saturated fats.

Sir John Hammond in the 1930s related the composition of animals to animal husbandry practices, but these were confined to relative amounts of protein and fat during growth, rather than nutritive aspects. However, this work established baselines on which to work, following the recent awareness by the producer of the cost effectiveness of reducing fat levels, and of the demand for leaner meat, on nutritional grounds, from the consumer. Considerable efforts are now being made to increase the ratio of protein to fat and of the ratio of unsaturated to saturated fat.

Breed selection of pigs for their ability to lay down protein and reduced fat levels has been intensive and highly successful; the level of back fat has reduced from 19 to 12mm in the past decade. The higher level of unsaturated fat in some cases can cause processing problems due to decreased fat firmness.

The decrease in the fat content of beef carcasses has been less dramatic but has certainly reduced with earlier slaughter weight and the introduction of the large lean continental breeds. Further increases have been achieved by the 'doppelender' or 'double-muscled' trait with its high protein to fat and unsaturated to saturated fat ratios.

Carcass compostion is also related to the sex of the animal. The male has a higher capacity to synthesise muscular tissue rather than fat. These differences apply equally well to cattle, sheep and pigs and there is now an increasing use of entire males in the industry.

The use of anabolic agents increases the proportion of protein and has been applied to males, females and castrates. These agents have now been banned on the basis of their residues in the meat, although, if the withdrawal period is properly applied, the levels are much less than the 'natural' hormone level of an animal. Alternative approaches to increasing the animal's own level of growth hormone, the use of beta- agonists, and the manipulation of the synthesis of fats are currently being researched, and may prove to be more acceptable.

Control may also be exercised by feed intake, not only the total intake but the nature of the intake. Thus the ingestion of unsaturated fatty acids by pigs will lead to increases in the proportion of unsaturated fat in the tissue. In cattle, sheep and goats the bacteria of the rumen hydrogenate unsaturated fatty acids, but this can be by-passed by encapsulation of the unsaturated fat feed in gelatin capsules. As can be seen from these examples, the possibilities of manipulating the nutritional value of the carcass are limited, apart from the direct method of reducing fat levels.

The major change in the near future in the supply of meat will be the increased leanness of animals primarily by breed and age, but also by a greater utilisation of male animals.

PROCESSING PRACTICES

Is the nutritive value of meat affected by processing practices? Curing is the use of salt for preserving fish and meat. The process usually involves addition of salt or sodium nitrate, the colour preserving properties of salt peter (nitrate) were probably due to impurities in the salt. Studies on the chemical reaction producing the colour, and the role of the bacteria in reducing nitrate to nitrite led to the direct use of nitrite, and hence to better control of both the preservative properties and the colour changes, It is also believed to improve the flavour.

Most of the innovations in curing, e.g. rapid methods by multi-needle injection, are of recent origin, within the last 30–40 years, and have increased the speed and distribution of the salt and facilitated mechanisation of the supply lines. Concern has been expressed in the reaction of nitrite to form nitrosamines, because of their carcinogenic properties, but the levels have been reduced dramatically and cured meat contains much less nitrate than vegetables and water. Additionally, the availability of home refrigerators has changed the emphasis to mild curing anyway and led to a wider variety of meat products.

The salting of comminuted meats led to the sausage, the work being derived from the Latin salsus which means preservation by salting. Today a variety of textures, flavours and shapes of sausage are available providing a large part of the meat processing industry.

Alkaline phosphates are often used in conjunction with curing salts. They are used primarily to decrease the amount of fluid lost during cooking. Their use is restricted to about 0.5% of the product weight. There is no evidence that they affect the nutritional value of the product, and in fact may increase it by preventing loss of nutrients in the cooking fluid.

Smoking of meat presumably has a similar long history as a method of preservation, as a colouring agent and to impart flavour. Its use was to reduce both the oxidative rancidity and the microbial population through the presence of phenols in the smoke which are potent bacteriostats and powerful antioxidants. Since smoke is confined to the surface of the product the activity of the phenols as preservatives is naturally concentrated on the surface. Surface coagulation caused by these compounds is critical in the development of the 'skinless' sausage. Liquid smoke is now often used for convenience, safety and economy. The liquid smoke contains polycyclic hydrocarbons, but most of the carcinogenic compounds are believed to be removed by this process. However, the importance of smoking has declined and it is only used in this mild form to increase variety in flavour and attractiveness.

ADDITIVES

Contrary to folk lore, additives do not represent a serious hazard. Nitrate and nitrosamines have acquired considerable notoriety but there is little evidence to support the claim that they are suspect. Other additives, flavour enhancers, antioxidants, colouring compounds, emulsifiers and stabilisers, have also been heavily criticised. The industry should certainly re-examine the use of the compounds, although the evidence is slight. As indicated earlier, removal of bacteriostats and antioxidants will be difficult and could be counter-productive against the consumer's and retailer's demand for convenience and shelf-life.

Substances formed during processing, lipid oxidation products and compounds produced through the Maillard reaction, have been shown to be carcinogenic in experimental animals. Similarly, cooking can produce 'burnt' products also believed to be mutagens, but their relevance to man needs to be fully assessed.

Yielding to the pressure for 'natural' products would reduce the product range, in addition to its palatability and attractiveness. A positive approach should be taken by the industry in catering for this small market for 'low additive' products and not a change in the whole product range.

NUTRITIONAL EFFECTS OF PROCESSING

The current emphasis on dietary goals by nutritionists, government and the general public has had its impact on the meat processing industry. It is clearly in the industry's interest to delineate the changes in nutrient quality due to processing. The major processes considered are, thermal processing, freezing, curing and smoking, dehydration and radiation. The effect of curing on the nutritive value of hams has been well studied and it appears that curing agents have little effect on the digestibility of the proteins or the bioavailability of the essential amino acids.

Thermal processing appears to be the only process in which significant changes in nutritive value occur. In general protein and fats are little affected; some vitamins, thiamin, B_6, B_{12} and pantothenic acid are heat-labile and significantly reduced (20–40%) during thermal processing. Niacin and riboflavin are generally unaffected. Minerals are also lost in the fluids exuded during cooking. Information on processed meats is fragmentary and incomplete and much more information is needed on the nutritional value of meat products.

The general conclusions must be that during processing some change in nutritional value occurs but this is slight as far as the major components of the meat are concerned. Significant loss of vitamins is incurred, but this is not excessive compared to normal domestic cooking procedures.

FUTURE PROCESSING TECHNOLOGY

The slow technological development of the meat industry, like that of other food industries, such as brewing, bread making and dairy products, is primarily due to the fact that it was initially craft based. It should not therefore be compared to the new chemical, petroleum and electronics industries since the new technology of the meat industry had to be based on improvements in the original craft industry. It is only very recently that the food industry has had to respond to the pressures of the market place and develop new processes, for example the Chorleywood Bread Process. The meat industry has a similar but more difficult job due to the highly variable nature of the raw material, and a lack of understanding of the most important properties of the meat affecting its suitability for the many different types of processing involved in the multitude of meat products produced.

The consumers' expectation for increased choice and fast food will accelerate the uptake of technology in the food industry. Over the past decade the number of large abattoirs has increased by 100% and these now take 60% of throughput, and to maintain efficiency are embracing new technology.

FRESH MEAT

Considerable effort is now being made to develop highly accurate and reproducible objective methods of evaluating carcass composition rather than the traditional visual methods. Non destructive fibre optic and ultrasonic probes have been developed and are now currently on trial to determine the amount and composition of the fat. Video image analysis is also being developed for continuous on-line monitoring of the fat content of carcasses. In the future carcass quality will be determined by a battery of on-line sensors feeding back data to a central computer. The carcass will then emerge with a tag containing all this data to provide an overall assessment of value.

Further processing techniques are being developed to ensure more consistent quality and greater throughput; for example, electrical stimulation and hot boning of carcasses and vacuum packing of the primals (large primary cuts), before refrigeration, is clearly cost effective. Electrical stimulation (100volts for two minutes) induces rapid rigor thereby avoiding variable toughening of the meat caused by rapid refrigeration. Refrigeration of boxes of boneless meat is obviously more efficient than the packing of ill-shaped carcasses containing a large proportion of bone. Electrical stimulation also has the advantage of reducing the conditioning time for holding meat in refrigeration and a consequently saving of energy.

The most dramatic change in the marketing of fresh meat has been the introduction of the modified atmosphere pack. The use of oxygen/carbon dioxide mixtures has ensured that the meat retains its consumer appeal in terms of bright red colour, whilst the carbon dioxide inhibits microbial growth and extends shelf-life.

MEAT PRODUCTS

In addition to providing more accurate data on the quality of meat for the fresh meat market, objective measurement of carcasses will provide important data for the meat processing industry. At the present time all processing operations have, of necessity, to be empirical since the factors governing the changes occurring are unknown.

Further data on chopped meat for processing is obtained by on-line determination of fat and lean content utilizing video image analysis (VIA). The method is rapid and accurate to 1% and therefore much more accurate and reliable than the human observer.

The development of alternative novel techniques will expand particularly in the high growth markets of ready meals and cook/chill. These will include high pressure cooking, vacuum cooking and microwave cooking. Currently attempts are being made to convert batch to continuous processes, which is becoming feasible as the processes themselves become less empirical.

This wide range of unit processes will have to be studied in terms of product safety as the consumer demand for changes, e.g. milder preservation, less salt etc increase. The industry will have to develop quality indicators for on-line monitoring and, perhaps more importantly, indicators of shelf-life as the traditional preservatives are removed.

A major innovation is the restructuring of meat which can involve the use of entire muscles or large muscle chunks as described earlier for the curing of hams, etc. For the purpose of this discussion restructuring will refer to the newer work on flaked meat. The restructuring of this material into uncured roasts or steaklets is currently expanding at a considerable rate as a convenience product. Considerable research has been carried out in this area to optimise bind and hence the texture of the product. The parameters involved vary from the comminution equipment, temperature of flaking, and variation of additives, to provide a variety of products. This area again shows demand for quality and value for money as well as convenience. The market for burgers is fairly static, whilst the restructured grillsteak area grew by 30% last year.

CONCLUSIONS

An ideal food should contain sufficient amounts of nutrients to cover all requirements of an individual for energy, protein, vitamins and minerals. No single food is capable of covering all the nutritional needs. However, meat is an excellent source of these components and if an individual had enough lean meat to eat, the requirements for most nutrients would be covered.

Meat and meat products provide a good balance of essential amino acids and are a good source of the B-complex vitamins. They are low, however, in the fat-soluble vitamins A, D, E and K and in vitamin C. Meat is a good source of phosphorus and iron, and contributes a significant number of minerals such as zinc, sodium, potassium, but is low in calcium. The biological value of meat is 75 compared to soya at 70.

Meat is often criticised as containing too much fat, generally quoted at 20% on the carcass but subsequent trimming reduces this value, and lean meat is actually less than 5% fat. The amount consumed is probably even less due to plate wastage by the consumer. At this level, the fat content of lean red meat is about the same as skinless poultry meat.

Knowledge of the nutritional value of the meat is believed to be of small influence in the choice of meat as a food, although there is a clear rejection of excess fat on health grounds and distaste. In the not too distant future, meat packaging labels will almost certainly offer full nutritional information. It must be recognised that people in developed countries eat meat primarily because they enjoy it, and believe it is good for them. This will no doubt continue in the foreseeable future.

To satisfy the need to provide good, fresh, lean meat of consistent quality the industry is paying greater attention to quality control. Variations in the product will erode the consumer's image of beef, for example, as a high-quality food. It must be remembered that the consumer cannot select at purchase in terms of flavour, tenderness or juiciness when cooked, and therefore needs information on quality that is consistent. The further demand for convenience and novelty of product requires increased processing of the meat. The technology of the industry is rapidly broadening to cope with this market pressure from the consumer.

The meat industry is very large, about £8 billion per year, constituting 27% of total food purchases, and can accept the challenge for lean cuisine by not only promoting meat as a good source of protein, calories and vitamins, but as a highly versatile and convenient food with a wide variety of products.

In the end analysis, meat is produced not to keep the industry going but to satisfy a consumer who wishes to eat meat. However, the business cannot be conducted on a volume price basis but must look to profitable new products. If the requirement is for lean meat, convenience foods, pre-cooked meals, etc then this is what the industry must produce if it is to survive as the major food commodity industry.

8
Fish and fish products
J. J. CONNELL

In the world league the British are average fish eaters. As an island nation strong in seafaring and surrounded by abundant fish stocks this might seem surprising, but our fish consumption has probably been determined by a number of factors, including competition from other foods produced here that are generally less available in comparable nations such as Japan and Iceland. Competition and availability certainly explain the relatively high British consumption of fish just after the last war and its steady decline until the late seventies (Table 1). Since then there has been a modest increase to about 7.5kg per head per annum. Indeed, since 1978 consumer expenditure on fish has risen more rapidly than for any other food (Stocker, 1987) but in total it is still only just over 3% of consumer expenditure on all foods (Sea Fish Industry Authority, 1983). There are several probable reasons why this reverse in fish consumption occurred. The first is a renewed interest in fish as an exotic gastronomic experience. We are all aware that nowadays fish very often features prominently in recipe books, restaurant menus and the food media. Secondly, the price of fish has managed to remain attractive despite difficulties over supplies. Thirdly, the larger fish processing companies have seen useful profit margins in fish and have maintained modest promotional campaigns on fish products. Also, for the last few years the development agency for the fish industry, the Sea Fish Industry Authority, has been running a new

Table 8.1   Changes in the British consumption of fish

Year	kg/person/year
1968	8.4
1970	7.8
1972	7.4
1974	6.4
1976	6.8
1978	6.3
1980	7.1
1982	7.4
1983	7.6
1984	7.2

national promotion campaign for fish along generic lines. According to the market analysts this campaign has heightened awareness of fish and stimulated more purchases. Fish manufacturers have responded to the more general trend for marketing added-value, ready-prepared dishes and meals, by incorporating more fish into them. Fish is becoming increasingly recognised as a food possessing specific health-giving benefits. Lastly, there is a current drive within the industry, particularly the chilled sector, to improve quality and presentation. Without denying that there is room for improvement, a recent report of poor freshness in fish (Consumers' Association, 1987) was based on small and unrepresentative samples; much larger, unpublished, surveys over the past few years of the freshness of both chilled and frozen fish by the Sea Fish Industry Authority and by Torry Research Station have shown that a much better standard is being achieved.

THE SPECIES MIX AND SUPPLIES

The most striking aspect of the use of fish and shellfish as food in Britain, as elsewhere, is the large number of species involved; about sixty are on regular sale here, though a relatively few, such as cod, haddock, plaice, mackerel, trout, salmon and scampi, dominate. Each species is the basis for a large number of different products. A recent count in representative retail outlets showed that the number of fish and shellfish products exceeded those made from beef, sheep meat, pork and chicken together.

As Table 2 (British Nutrition Foundation, 1986) shows, the amounts of fish caught do not necessarily correspond to those consumed. For example, most mackerel caught is exported or converted into fish meal and oil; conversely, about half the cod eaten is imported. About 1.1 million tonnes of gutted weight of fish and shellfish, both home caught and imported, are used for British consumption.

Table 8.2   The major fish species caught and eaten in 1984

Species	Annual UK Catch [a, b]	Edible weight available for human consumption in the UK [c]
Mackerel	200	17
Cod	114	85
Haddock	110	49
Herring	73	15
Whiting	61	18
Sand eels	48	—
Plaice	26	17
Scampi	22	10

[a] Landed weight (gutted) in thousands of tonnes
[b] British vessels only
[c] Including imports; thousands of tonnes

Because of conservatism of eating habits, individual representatives of the species mix change only slowly with time, the last major addition being scampi about 30 years ago. There are, however, important changes over time in the quantities of the representatives. For example, the consumption of herring was reasonably high until about 15 years ago. At that time a dearth of supplies occurred through European governments banning fishing in many traditional areas because of the alarmingly low state of stocks. The recent resumption of controlled fishing for herring has given rise to a slow increase in consumption, stimulated by advertising campaigns. Nevertheless, current consumption of herring is still much less than it was. Another example is mackerel, which was hardly eaten up to about 20 years ago. Around that time a vast increase in mackerel catching occurred and efforts were made to open up markets for the species in Britain. These efforts were partially successful, as the widespread availability of hot smoked mackerel and mackerel pate shows. Squid is a similar case, in that, at times, significant quantities are caught but almost all of it has to be exported. Another example, in the reverse direction, is cod. Up to about 20 years ago the amounts of this species caught and eaten were roughly in balance. As a result of British fishermen being almost completely excluded from traditional distant water fishing grounds, supplies of home-caught cod fairly rapidly diminished. To meet continued high demand, cod has had to be imported in large quantities. A further consequence, however, has been a search for alternative supplies of white-flesh species that could be reasonably substituted for cod in products such as fish finger and portions. Today, therefore, depending upon availability and price, modest quantities of a variety of suitable species are imported for this purpose including for example, South American hake, Alaska pollock, and blue whiting. Because they are incorporated into manufactured products these species are not usually identified as such. Small quantities of exotic species are also increasingly imported, mainly for the use of ethnic communities.

A significant contribution to new supplies has been made in recent years by farmed trout and salmon. Estimated British productions of these fish in 1987 were 12 000 and 16 000 tonnes respectively (*Fish Farming International*,1987; *Fish Farmer*,1987). Production of farmed salmon in Scotland is estimated to rise to 25 000 tonnes in 1988. In addition, relatively small quantities of farmed trout, salmon and mussels are imported, and there is some small home production of farmed oysters, mussels and scallops. At present the costs of farming fish can only be met from relatively high priced species that lend themselves to husbandry, though experiments with common, lower priced, species, such as cod, are taking place.

The immediate prospects for British-caught wild supplies is less bright than for farmed species. EEC quotas for most white-fleshed species and for mackerel have been reduced for 1987 and the position is unlikely to change much for 1988. Some shellfish stocks are under pressure. Thereafter, it is hoped that increased biological productivity and tight fishing controls will allow higher catches to be restored. Because demand is high and likely to remain so, the main consequence of these shortfalls is likely to be more imports. There are a number of species available to British vessels that are not fully exploited on the home market, and new attempts are being made to utilise them. These species include herring and mackerel, as already mentioned, small haddock and whiting, argentines, blue whiting, pout and crab. Success will, however, depend on the introduction of new economically viable processing technologies and new products, research on which is continuing.

PROCESSING AND PRODUCTS

A summary of the main types and relative proportions of products sold in shops and used in catering outlets is shown in Table 3. There are also a number of important products for manufacturing, such as the, so-called, laminated block, but these will not be discussed. It should be noted that some products sold chilled or cooked may have been frozen up to the point of sale.

Within the chilled or fresh category, some products such as iced, 'wet' fish, shellfish and smoked fish are very traditional and have not changed for decades. Sales of these traditional forms have declined steadily since the last war but appear now to be stabilising. This decline is attributed mainly to changing shopping habits and preferences for flesh foods that are easily handled and prepared. Sales of kippers, which are a cold-smoked product, have also declined, partly because of shortages of supplies and partly

Table 8.3   Main types of retail or catering fish products

Product groups	Approximate percentage of total sales	Examples
Chilled, fresh or cooked	50	'wet' or iced whole or gutted fish 'wet' or iced fillets or steaks 'wet' or iced shellfish cooked shellfish breaded and/or battered fish and shellfish, including catering products smoked fish prepacked/gas packed fish and fillets recipe dishes shellfish analogue products
Frozen	35	individual quick frozen or inter leaved fillets and shellfish breaded and/or battered fish and shellfish, including fish fingers and portions smoked fish recipe dishes
Canned, bottled and semi-preserved	15	salmon tuna, sardines etc in oil or tomato marinades and salads patés, spreads, etc bottled shellfish

because of the decline in cooked breakfasts. In contrast hot-smoked mackerel, which is a new, convenient and tasty product, is now sold in substantial amounts. Coated fillets and shellfish, being variants of the traditional fish 'cake', have enjoyed a modest success. Major growth in this category has occurred, however, with the last three in the list shown in Table 3. In line with trends in packaging technology for fresh meat and poultry, pre-packaging in air and vacuum, and modified atmosphere packing of fish products, have experienced a resurgence. Most of these products are sold in multiple shops. The reasons for their growth include suitability for multiple retailing, attractiveness of the packaging styles, enhanced shelf life and convenience for shopping and storage. Whether they will continue to grow in popularity is unclear because they are unlikely to displace most of the traditional forms of presentation. An increased number and variety of ready prepared dishes such as moules marinières and fish salads are being marketed, again mainly through the multiples. The relatively high price of these products, which offer useful vehicles for adding value to the raw material, has not deterred purchasing so far. One of the most interesting developments in chilled products is the shellfish analogue. These are realistic simulations of shellfish meat, such as crab leg meat, made by a variant of the ancient Japanese product, kamaboko or fish jelly. Although based on intrinsically weak tasting white fish flesh, the appearance, taste and texture of the finished products are all close to those of the natural article. The manufactured products are frozen but they are usually presented for sale in the chilled or partly thawed state. Originally they were made in Japan and exported to North America and Europe, but more recently production has been established outside Japan, including one factory at Motherwell, Scotland. British sales annually are currently several million pounds value. The importance of these products lies in the fact that low cost, white fish raw material, much of it unsaleable as such, is being converted into a product of much higher price and demand. Unlike the situation with the carcass meats industry, which has introduced many re-formed products, the fish industry has lagged behind in this type of technology. Further growth is, however, likely as more ingenious new simulations of fish and shellfish are found. There would be considerable advantages if abundant, dark-fleshed, fatty species such as mackerel, herring and sprat could be converted through kamaboko or other technologies into high quality analogues; much research is currently under way on this largely unsolved problem.

In addition to those already indicated, technical developments in the chilled sector could include combined treatments to extend shelf life and to improve presentation. Combinations of gas packing, skin packing, chemical preservatives, pasteurisation and sterilisation are likely to be used. Because of benefits from extension of shelf lives and reduction of risks from pathogens, fish and shellfish are prime candidates for irradiation treatment, but the future for this technology is strongly linked, of course, to the uncertain future of food irradiation generally.

The frozen fish category for the past 20 or 30 years has grown steadily and the industrial view is that, despite some difficulties in the last year or so, there is still potential for growth (*Fish Trader*, 24 May 1986; *Frozen Food Management*, 1987). Currently, frozen fish contributes 25–30 per cent to all frozen food products. The mainstays of the frozen fish market remain coated fish fingers, portions and related products, and some growth here is still possible through the introduction of products with new coatings including those higher in fibre. Demand for IQF shellfish continues to be high. However, the main growth has been, and is likely to be, in so-called recipe or ready-prepared dishes such as fish in a wide variety of sauces, fish and chips, and whole meals. Fish features prominently in health-conscious brand lines and 'calorie-counted' dishes suitable for microwave cooking are also providing a useful vehicle for different fish species. In total a large range is already available and the list is growing because manufacturers and food technologists see much more scope for exploiting the versatility of fish and shellfish. Again, many of these new products are relatively high priced, at least for fish products generally. Almost all are based on white fish or shellfish. As already pointed out, supply of these species present some difficulties. What would be extremely useful to the fish industry is the development of ranges of convenience products based on the abundant dark-fleshed, fatty species. In the past, products such as herring or kipper fingers have been trial marketed without sustained success, but because of the large rewards, research on such products is still being pursued to find the right combination of technology, gastronomic attractiveness to consumers, and price. Alleviation of the problem of supply of conventional white fish could come from the use of unconventional species. Unfortunately many of these are small in size and the fillets obtained from them are insufficiently large to be incorporated as such in most high quality convenience products. A few years ago Torry Research Station made one technological contribution here by devising means of coalescing small fillets into large pieces possessing the main characteristics of larger fillets. The process was eventually commercialised on a limited scale. The commercial versions suffered, however, from a failure to completely retain fillet-like structure in the finished product. Recent developments at Torry on a new machine appear to overcome this difficulty.

Unlike the declining situation with canned foods generally, sales in recent years of canned and heat processed fish have shown a modest increase in both volume and value (Connell,1987). No ready explanation for this phenomenon is available, though it may be connected with the fact that canned fish such as pilchards offer one of the cheapest forms of protein. Furthermore, there has been a recent increase on the market of spreadable products made from fish.

FISHING PORTS AND CENTRES OF PROCESSING

The drastic decline in distant water fishing has led to the virtual demise of Hull as a fishing port; for many years it held premier position. For the same reason Grimsby has also declined but is sustained by a greater proportion of North Sea landings. Despite these changes a good deal of fish is now transported to the Humberside ports from Iceland, Scotland and the East coast of England. For this reason and because of the major capital investment there, Humberside remains one of the two main centres of processing. The other main centre is the North East of Scotland where landings from inshore and middle waters have kept up or increased somewhat. Scotland has also benefited from the Motherwell factory mentioned earlier, and major factories for the processing of pelagic species are mooted near Invergordon and in the Shetlands. Major changes in the location of the main processing centres are unlikely in the foreseeable future.

DISTRIBUTION, RETAILING AND CATERING

Most fish of all kinds is distributed inland by road. Minor quantities go by rail and air. Most chilled fish is distributed from processors at the ports to wholesale inland markets such as Billingsgate in London and thence to retailers and caterers. From Humberside a significant proportion of chilled fish by-passes the inland markets (*Fishing News International*, 1987). Frozen fish is distributed along with other frozen foods.

As will be obvious to most people, the major change in retailing over the past few decades has been the drastic decline in the number of traditional fishmongers. For example, over the past 10 years it is estimated that their numbers have fallen by about 20% and the amount of chilled fish sold through them by about 50%. Currently, there is only one fishmonger per 19 000 people, a very concerning figure for the industry. The reasons for the decline are changes in shopping habits, unfamiliarity among young people with traditional forms of fish, and the shortfall in iced cod supplies. At the same time, by skilful and vigorous promotion and presentation many fishmongers are highly successful.

Luckily, this decline has been countered by a significant growth in sales of chilled fish by mutiple retailers who recognise the commodity as a high profit sector. At present only about 10% of multiples sell chilled fish but this proportion is likely to increase as the processing sector adjusts to meeting the special and demanding product requirements of the major retailers. Sales of frozen and canned fish are well taken care of through the established outlets such as the multiples, freezer centres, co-ops and grocers.

The quantity of fish sold through catering outlets is surprisingly high and almost the same as that bought for home consumption (Cormack, 1986). Traditional fried fishshops, now supplemented by franchised take-away shops, are holding their own and currently it is estimated that they distribute about 18% of all fish consumed in Britain. It seems that there is a very stable social need for this kind of product. At the same time some of their persistence is attributable to diversification into other ready-cooked foods.

NUTRITIONAL ASPECTS

Protein

Fish contribute about 5% to total protein consumption, which is about the same as the 7% contributed by beef (British Nutrition Foundation,1986). The amino acid compositions of all the fish and shellfish species eaten are very similar to those of flesh foods generally. In dietary texts the easy digestibility of fish flesh is often commented upon. Whilst there is little experimental evidence for this view, the relatively low connective tissue content of fish flesh and the low conversion temperature of fish collagen into gelatin would certainly lend it support.

Chilling, freezing and storage in the frozen state have little or no effect on the nutritional quality of fish protein. Small amounts of protein can be lost in drip or leached during icing. One report of decreases in certain protein-bound amino acids during frozen storage (Kolakowski *et al.*,1972) has not been substantiated.

Cooking in water or canning have, at worst, only marginal deleterious effects on the nutritional value of fish protein (Aitken and Connell, 1977). Frying of fish under normal conditions can result in moderate losses of available lysine (Tooley and Lawrie, 1974), but a full evaluation of the implications for nutritional value of this method of cooking has not been made. The same is true of the effects of smoking.

Lipids

The lipid content, and consequently energy value, of fish varies greatly with season when the fish is caught. Lean fish, like cod, have as little as 0.7% lipid and offer nutritionalists and dieticians a useful source of low-fat food. In fatty fish, like mackerel, lipid content can vary from 1% to over 30%.

Fish lipids differ from those of land animals and of plants in possessing much higher proportions of highly unsaturated fatty acids. By 'highly' is meant containing more than three double bonds. The main consequence is that fish lipids are relatively prone to oxidative rancidity, sometimes with unpleasant effects on sensory quality. As a result, the storage lives of fish products, particularly those made from fatty species, are often less than those of other flesh foods under the same conditions. Many fish products require special protection, such as packaging or glazing, if they are to be stored for long periods. Doubts about the safety of eating highly oxidised lipids have been expressed, but the generality of processing conditions to which British fish products are subjected do not, in fact, result in appreciable lipid oxidation. It is very unlikely, therefore, that British consumers are at health risk from this effect.

There is, however, one important positive nutritional consequence of the polyunsaturated nature of fish lipids. Some epidemiological evidence suggests that increasing the proportion of fish in the diet may protect against coronary heart disease, and possibly other disease (Nettleton, 1985; British Nutrition Foundation, 1986; Lands, 1986; Seafood International, 1986). Biochemical and clinical evidence suggests that the key factor may not be the quantity *per se* of the polyunsaturated acids in fish lipids but their unique nature. Fish polyunsaturated acids are predominantly of the linolenic series which is characterised by having a double bond in the n-3 position in the hydrocarbon backbone. These relatively recent findings have led to a great deal of new research on the possible beneficial effects of eating fish, the results of which are naturally awaited with keen interest by the fish industry. Already, however, they are having a positive impact on demand for fish in many countries, including Britain. Fatty fish, which are particularly rich in n-3 acids, are currently not easy to sell, as already pointed out, but this nutritional information is likely to have a marked positive influence on demand for them.

Another off-shoot of this matter has been the growth in the manufacture of fractions or concentrates of fish oils which are richer in n-3 acids than the oils themselves. Such preparations are sold pharmaceutically, usually in capsule form, as protectants against heart disease. Most medical authorities, however, caution against their indiscriminate and uncontrolled use.

Vitamins

The content of all vitamins in lean fish and shellfish is very similar to that of carcass meats (British Nutrition Foundation,1986). Fatty fish on the other hand are high in the fat-soluble vitamins A and D; they are the best natural source of the latter. Also, the livers of all fish are particularly high in vitamins A and D. Although fish livers are seldom eaten as such, the extracted oils are used as supplements to the diet.

Under the relatively mild conditions to which most British fish products are subject, losses of vitamins will be small or negligible (British Nutrition Foundation, 1986). Moderate losses of thiamine and other B vitamins occur during canning. Because fish is not a main contributor to the vitamin content of the British diet, none of the losses are nutritionally significant.

Minerals

The mineral composition of fish flesh is, with two exceptions, very similar to that of carcass meats and its contribution to the diet correspondingly similar. The exceptions are iodine and selenium, for which fish and marine products generally are good and useful sources.

Some canned fish products, and smoked and marinated products from pelagic species, contain substantial amounts of edible bone and therefore they provide good sources of calcium and phosphorus.

Leaching causes some depletion of mineral content in whole fish held for long periods in melting ice. In the opposite direction, brining for smoking, pickling or canning substantially increases the sodium and chloride content of fish. Although their use has decreased recently, poly-phosphates are still used fairly extensively in the manufacture of products such as fish fingers and portions. This gives rise to enhanced contents of sodium and phosphorus. There is no evidence or expectation, however, that these shifts in mineral content have any significant nutritional effect.

Additives and standards

In response to consumer demands there has been some recent movement towards reduction in the use of some additives in fish products. The extent of this movement is impossible to quantify and thus only subjective observations are possible at this time.

The case of polyphosphates has just been noted, the motivation being the need to avoid additives for which there seems to be no overwhelming technological justification. A few major retailers now require that fish products sold in their shops contain no azo or artificial dyes, of which brown FK, the material traditionally used to colour kippers, is the prime example. Fish is either being smoked without added colour or is being treated with natural colours such as annato or crocein rather than azo dyes.

Somewhat in the opposite direction is the case of sulphites. Until about six years ago, no fish or shell fish product could be treated with these substances in Britain. The prohibition was then removed to bring Britain in line with practice in the rest of the EEC. As a result a rather small proportion of British crab, prawn and scampi are now being treated. The objective is to protect against the enzymic blackening that can adversely affect the meat of some of these crustacea.

Many smoked fish products, in common with other smoked foods, contain mutagenic substances such as polycyclic aromatic hydrocarbons. Because of this, concern has been expressed about risks to health from eating smoked fish, which is one of the principal smoked foods eaten in Britain. The amounts of possibly toxic materials are, however, very small indeed and no greater than in several other common foods. Nevertheless, there has been a small movement away from conventional smoking techniques towards the use of smoke flavouring solutions which have been specially treated to remove polycyclic aromatic hydrocarbons.

In response to concerns expressed over the last few years, by those representing the interests of consumers about certain aspects of composition, the Food Advisory Committee earlier this year produced a report on coated and ice-glazed fish products. They recommended (Food Advisory Committee, 1987) a number of new requirements, the most important of which are:

> Fish fingers coated with batter and breadcrumbs should contain not less than 55% and 60% of fish, respectively.

> Other coated products do not need to be regulated by compositional standards.

> All coated fish products should bear a fish content declaration.

> All glazed fish products should bear an indication of the net weight of fish core prior to glazing.

These recommendations, on which comments have been solicited, are designed to offer greater protection to consumers than exists at present.

TECHNOLOGICAL DEVELOPMENTS IN FISH HAND-LING AND PROCESSING

In addition to those already noted, a number of other important developments should be mentioned briefly.

On fishing vessels a good deal of recent progress has been made and will continue to be made on the introduction of a greater degree of mechanical handling, involving, for example, sorting tables, conveyors, washing machines, gutting machines and robust weighing scales. The objectives are to reduce the manual content of operations, to improve efficiency and economics and to improve quality. Coupled with these developments is the slow but inexorable replacement of wooden boxes and fixings by plastic equipment. About 25 years ago a major revolution took place in the British fishing fleet with the introduction of freezing at sea. Nearly 50 large, freezing at sea, trawlers were eventually in service. Today, as a result of the expulsion of British fisherman from distant water grounds, only two or three vessels of this kind continue fishing. Interestingly, however, there has been a resurgence of interest in freezing at sea, but this time using medium-sized trawlers which freeze only part of the catch. One such vessel is being designed, probably for operation from a Scottish port.

An interesting development at port markets is the application of refrigeration to chill part of the new facilities at Fraserburgh. Such systems exist in Europe but this is the first in Britain. Again the objective is to maintain quality by keeping temperatures low during discharge, auction and delays before removal from the market.

In factories, the main change, over the past years, has again been the use of more mechanical handling, and in some cases of microelectronic controlled equipment such as computers, automatic weighing and packing machines, graders and smoking kilns. More efficient freezers for fillets and small shellfish are also being introduced.

Until recently there has been a move towards the greater use of mechanically recovered fish flesh, but this now seems to be slackening. More flesh undoubtedly could be removed from skeletons after filleting or from small fish but its quality is low, and so far no way of improving most of it has been found. Research is, however, continuing on the problem of upgrading.

Throughout the fish industry there is a growing recognition that quality and presentation must be improved if fish is to compete effectively with other foods. This feeling is being given practical expression by the important efforts of the development body for the industry, the Sea Fish Industry Authority, who have mounted a number of quality campaigns including approved quality marks for fishmongers and codes of practice. Individual companies and trade associations are also introducing more quality assurance schemes. In most cases these initiatives involve technical advice on how new quality objectives can be achieved through changes in practices.

CONCLUSIONS

Judged generally the fish industry has entered a period of guarded optimism. Fish is perceived by consumers and publicists as having a number of important positive features. Consumption has grown in recent years and demand is good. The added-value product range has expanded considerably and there is further scope for diversification. Some catching sectors are buoyant. There is concern about home-caught supplies, particularly from small processors in Aberdeen who have experienced some decline in business in recent years. The major processors, however, seem to be able to hold their own as far as supplies are concerned. A reasonable amount of investment in new technology and equipment is taking place. Promotion of fish is being boosted from its previously very low level. Nutritionally, fish makes a modest contribution to the British diet which could become more important if present indications about health benefits are confirmed. Changes in processing and products are unlikely to have major nutritional implications, though recent dietary recommendations are having, and will continue to have, an effect on the kinds of fish products offered.

References

Aitken, A. and Connell, J. J. (1979). In Priestley, R. J. (ed.) *Effects of heating on foodstuffs.* p.219-54, (Applied Science Publishers, London)

British Nutrition Foundation (1986). *Nutritional aspects of fish.* Briefing paper no 10

Connell, J. J. (1987). New developments in the marketing of fish. *Food Marketing*, 3, 118-29

Consumers' Association Ltd (1987). Report on Fish. *Which*, May, 225

Cormack, K. (1986). Sea Fish Industry Authority, private communication

Fish Farmer (1987), Mackay salutes a £60M industry. 10, No2, 23

Fish Farming International (1987), Promotion boosts British trout. 14, No.3, 4

Fish Trader (1986), Convenience food boom. 24 May, 7

Fishing News International (1987), Researcher takes close look at British fish market chain. 26, No.1, 36

Food Advisory Committee (1987). *Report on coated and ice-glazed fish products*. (HMSO, London)

Frozen Food Management (1987). Fish supplies - affecting frozen prices. January/February, pp.24-8

International Union of Food Science and Technology/International Union of Nutritional Science (1987). *The effect of smoking and drying on the nutritional properties of fish*. Burt, J. R. (ed.)

Kolakowski, E., Fik, M. and Karminska, S. (1972). Investigations into changes in the protein nutritive value of frozen fish sausages produced from fresh and frozen minced flesh. *Bull. Intern. Inst. Refrig.* Annex 2, 59

Lands, W. E. M. (1986). *Fish and human health.* (Academic Press, London)

Nettleton, J. A. (1985). *Seafood nutrition.* (Osprey Books, London)

Sea Fish Industry Authority (1983). *Marketing British fish* (Sea Fish Industry Authority, Edinburgh)

Seafood International (1986). Seafood and health. They go together. February, 15

Stocker, T. (1987). Food manufacture in the UK: current and perceived trends. In Turner, A. (ed.) *Food technology international.* p.14. (Sterling Publications Ltd., London)

Tooley, P. J. and Lawrie, R. A. (1974). Effect of deep fat frying on the availability of lysine in fish fillets. *J. Fd Technol.*, 9, 247

9
Oils and fats

R. W. HUNT

The manufacture, production and processing of oils and fats goes back a long way, and has been a mix of rapid innovation, legislative restriction, stagnant development, and nutritional debate. Above all it has been a history of consumer demand and the design modification of products to meet that demand. If we go back far enough, the first real breakthrough was the farmer who made butter, by churning sweet fresh cream, to spread on his bread, rather than use the renderings from beef, pork or sheep, to provide the flavour and lubrication during eating which is the desirable consumer benefit. The butter was not much of a product–it did not keep very well, it weeped the water phase, went very hard in the cold and very soft and runny when warmed. Certainly it did not travel very well and anyone without their own source of milk probably had to make do with the renderings from the roast meat. Even the addition of salt (was that the first food additive?) did not do a lot to improve the keeping quality.

Of course, for an army on the move, the supply of food must have been difficult, and the supply of butter must have been very spasmodic. It may well have been a concern for the rank and file that led Napoleon III to offer a prize for the invention of a butter substitute but more probably it was a shortage of non-rancid butter in the Imperial caravan that was a more pressing need. In any event the challenge was taken up, and the prize won by the invention of a French chemist, Mege Mouries. The original product was made from cow udder fat, no doubt a valiant attempt to get close to the real thing, and since that time the fat phase of such products has included just about every animal fat and vegetable fat that has been available.

It would appear that the first vegetable oils to be used in margarine manufacture were palm kernel and coconut oil, both from West Africa in the later 19th century, when a Mr F. W. Loder made margarine from these fats. Development work was necessary before palm oil could be used.

As in Europe, margarines began to be produced in the US and again flourished because they met the consumer demand for a product that was cheaper than butter and also a product which kept better than the butters of the day, which were often rancid by the time they were sold in towns.

At that time there was no substitute for the other so-called natural fat – lard – either in the US or in Europe and again it needed a chemist, this time a German research scientist named Normann to invent a process, hydrogenation, in the 1920s, to enable oils and fats to be made harder. The commercial exploitation of the Normann invention took place in the UK and also in the US where there was an abundant supply of liquid cottonseed oil – a by-product from the thriving cotton industry. In the late 1920s Proctor and Gamble first hydrogenated cottonseed oil in the US to produce a 'substitute lard' with good performance and keeping quality, under the brand name Crisco, which still thrives today.

The invention and subsequent development of hydrogenation was the key step that has enabled the shortening and oil industry worldwide to move ahead and develop a whole range of products, with reliable, constant performance and good keeping qualities, from extremely wide and variable oil sources.

Today, margarines and shortenings, be they for conventional spread usage, or with low fat content, or high in polyunsaturated content for nutritional reasons, or for making puff pastry in the food processing industry, will require vastly different formulations. They will be made from a very wide selection of oils from animal, marine oil or vegetable oil stocks ranging from the relatively saturated palm oil to soyabean oil, cottonseed, groundnut, rapeseed and sunflower and many other minor oils.

The oils used have also varied widely over the years and the ability to handle the economic oil stock of the day has been one of the major learning points of the industry, in order to provide the most economical formulae possible. Between 1938 and 1954 the major change was the increased usage of palm oil. After decontrol of margarine manufacture in 1954 the use of groundnut, cottonseed, and coconut declined rapidly and the use of marine oil began to grow. There is a further change hidden in these figures in that up to the late '50s the marine oil used was whale oil, whereas, since then, the use of herring and other fish oil has totally replaced whale. This apparently small change in fact involved the industry in major technical effort to be able to hydrogenate the highly unstable marine oil, in order to achieve oxidative stability in the finished margarine.

Before going on to discuss the processing requirements of the various crude oils an understanding of the fatty acid make up of the various oils is interesting. The edible oils from both animal and vegetable sources are triglycerides, that is a glycerol molecule substituted with three fatty acid chains. Essentially it is the length and make up of the chains which control the features of the triglyceride, and the crude oils vary widely in fatty acid content. The chains are defined according to the number of carbon atoms and double bonds occurring.

There are large differences in these fatty acid chains, and their distribution, particularly between the relatively unsaturated vegetable and marine oils compared to the more saturated triglycerides such as tallow fat. Some vegetable oils (notably palm oil, palm kernel oil and coconut oil) contain higher percentages of saturates compared to seed oils such as sunflower, soya and rapeseed.

The different fatty acid patterns makes each oil distinctive and different processing may be necessary before the oil can be used in margarine or shortening.

The processes used in the manufacturing of these products can be divided into four major steps:

(1) Purifying the crude oil.
(2) Modifying the characteristics of the oil.
(3) Blending.
(4) Plasticisation and packing.

The first two concern processing the oil alone, the third is the basic process controlling finished product performance and the fourth group transforms the required oil blend into the finished product for packing.

PURIFYING

The first of the purifying processes is commonly called refining or neutralising during which the major contaminant, free fatty acid, is neutralised, generally with caustic soda added stoichemetrically, after which the resultant soap is washed from the oil stream. Historically this process was carried out on a batch basis dating from about 1880 but today almost all refining is done with continuous equipment. An option, which is becoming more popular, particularly for very good quality vegetable oils, is to use a physical refining process. Physical refining removes impurities with a combination of vacuum and steam stripping, but for many oils chemical refining is still necessary.

The next stage of the purification process is to remove coloured compounds by bleaching the oil with an activated earth which, of course, is then later removed by filtration. Again this bleaching and filtration process now regularly uses continuous equipment, rather than the batch equipment of some years ago. It was the development of bleaching technology which allowed the use of palm oil earlier this century. At that time the colour of palm oil was very dark, and without bleaching was not suitable for use.

The final purifying stage is deodorisation of the oil, and while it will be described here, it is not normally carried out until any hydrogenation and fat blending has been completed. Deodorising, as the name implies, is aimed at removing odorous compounds, and other non triglycerides, which have survived earlier processing. In practice, many other undesirable components are stripped during the process, which is carried out at high temperatures under vacuum, with stripping steam aiding the volatilisation of the undesirables. Again, earlier equipment carried out the process on a batch basis but modern equipment is based on a continuous or at the least semi-continuous process. The importance of this final stage cannot be over emphasised. It is a key process in guaranteeing the bland flavour and ageing stability which are prerequisite for any fat-based food product.

Thus, at the end of the purification stages, we have a blend of oils or a single stock, from which all traces of free fatty acid, colour, ordorous compounds and many other compounds which are not pure triglyceride, have been removed, although it should be added that the purification processes do not affect the degree of saturation or chain lengths of the fatty acids.

Deodorisation is the final stage of purification processing and is usually carried out after the particular blend of oil has been prepared. Blending is necessary because of the tremendously wide range of fat-based products which the housewife or the food manufacturer requires. Many of these have quite different properties, because the job they are required to do can vary widely.

At one time, all blends for making margarine were probably similar, but today there are so many different types of margarine, all with different consumer benefits to deliver, that they require different types of oil blend. It is important to choose the correct oil formula to give the desired finished product.

This, of course, is in addition to the obvious requirement that the oil blend should be totally stable, in order to resist the onset of oxidation, hydrolysis or any of the degradation reactions which lead to rancidity, off flavour and a loss of consumer acceptability. Margarine oils have to withstand the presence of a water phase in intimate contact with oil. Baking margarines have to withstand the accelerative effect of baking temperatures and, even then, many have to provide good stability in the baked product for six months or longer. Yet again, in the design of frying oils it is the stability of the oil at 180°C which is important although it is still important that the oil in the potato crisp, having survived the onslaught of oxidative reactions at 180°C must then remain flavour stable in the packet of crisps for 12 weeks or more.

All of these basic product requirements influence the choice of oil blend which the formulator will select, to provide the required performance characteristics that the finished user requires, either in the home or the food processing factory. To formulate adequately 'building blocks' of various oils, made to varying degrees of hardness, are necessary.

The key analytical tool of the shortening and oil chemist is the 'solids profile'. Years ago, this was measured at a series of temperatures across the usage range by a dilatation technique, but nowadays it is almost exclusively measured using nuclear magnetic resonance (NMR) techniques, which can provide the information very rapidly and accurately. The solids content of the fat blend is measured at temperatures ranging from 10°C upwards and most importantly at mouth or blood temperature.

The blends must be made from a range of crude oils, that is either animal fats, or marine oils, or vegetable oils such as soyabean, palm, rapeseed, or sunflowerseed possibly with other oils such as cottonseed, or palm kernel. In order to achieve the flexibility of formulation necessary and to avoid the necessity of using one particular oil which may suddenly rise in price on a worldwide commodity market, the product formulator needs to arm himself with a range of stocks from these crude oils to produce the required blends.

MODIFICATION

This is where the second group of processing techniques come in, with the objective of making the appropriate building blocks from the crudes available.

The first of these is hydrogenation. Hydrogenation is the process by which hydrogen is added directly to points of unsaturation in the fatty acids. The purpose of the process is firstly to harden the oil by elimination of double bonds, in order to convert liquid oils to a semi solid form, and secondly, to improve the oxidative stability of the oil, by elimination of the more highly unsaturated fatty acids. The most convenient analysis to measure the degree of unsaturation is the Iodine Value. High Iodine Values indicate a liquid, or unsaturated oil, whilst the harder solid fats have low IV. It is important to recognise that hydrogenation can be used to harden an oil all the way to a solid fat with an iodine value of below 5, or to 'touch hydrogenate' the oil so that the triple bond unsaturates are reduced, to improve stability, without making the oil much harder. In order to have the right stocks for blending one may use three or more different degrees of hydrogenation of a given crude oil in order to provide the stocks necessary for flexibility of formulation.

The hydrogenation process has traditionally been carried out as a batch reaction. This was necessarily very slow, since the catalyst and hydrogen were introduced after heating the oil to the appropriate temperature. Once the reaction started, being exothermic, it was controlled by the skills of the operator in either restricting hydrogen, cooling the oil via the coils used for heating, or altering the pressure in the reactor. It took a great deal of skill to stop the reaction at the correct end point in order to ensure product of the correct hardness. This was particularly true since the important parameters of solid content and iodine value were relatively slow analyses and the completeness of the reaction was therefore judged on the refractive index of the oil which gives an indication of iodine value.

There are now semi-continuous plants available from equipment manufacturers which, as well as improving control, also provide the opportunity of using the heat of reaction to heat incoming oil and are generally much more energy efficient. At Procter and Gamble, we use a company-designed hydrogenation reactor, which is truly continuous and in which a reaction, that could take hours in a batch process, is accomplished in minutes, through a single-pass agitated-column reactor. The flexibility of this equipment is such that it can be used to 'touch hydrogenate', for example, rapeseed oil through a drop in iodine value of 20 units and to hydrogenate marine oil hard enough to achieve stability through an iodine value drop of 80 units.

A different process which again aims at providing hard and soft versions of a given oil is the process of fractionation. This can be done simply by letting the oil stand at a suitably low temperature when the harder component will crystallise and settle out (the stearic fraction) with the softer olein fraction remaining. This process is known as dry fractionation or winterisation. Other fractionaction processes, based on solvent or detergent fractionation are also available which can be tuned to give the hardness of oil required. Fractionation is not so flexible a process as hydrogenation, since it is really only useful with the harder oils, such as palm or tallow.

A third modification process that can also alter the hardness of an oil, and particularly its crystallisation characteristics, is the process of interesterification. In effect, what this means is that the fatty acids on the glycerol backbone are released and randomly reassigned, either using a single oil, or blends of oils, to produce a fat with the desired hardness. The position of a fatty acid on the glyceride molecule can have a distinct effect on the melting point of the triglyceride, particularly if an unsaturated fatty acid is moved from the two position to either the one or the three positions. The interesterification reaction is generally carried out at relatively low temperatures with the addition of suitable catalysts, by batch processing.

PRODUCT FORMULATION

Thus, at the end of this processing, oil stocks, or building blocks are available from any of the currently available crudes, with hardnesses ranging from the unhardened soft oil to three or more different hardnesses of oil. Each stock will have its own characteristic solids curve through the usage temperature range, and the formulator can choose how best to achieve the required solids curve for the oil blend of his finished product. Quite often, the solids at different temperatures are additive, but with some oils there are solubility effects which often make the blending job a subject of trial and error.

To give an example, an ordinary cooking margarine may require a solids curve at $10/20/35°C$ of $50/25/5$. This may be achieved with a blend of three different marine stocks in the ratios $20:30:50$. Alternatively a vegetable based product may use different vegetable stocks to meet the same solids requirement and performance. A puff pastry margarine might have a solids requirement of $60/50/20$ at $10°C/20°C/35°C$ and again could be made from the same stock as the cooking margarine but in different proportions.

Consumer demand has led the industry from the position where one margarine formulation and one shortening formulation would cover all consumer requirements, to a position today where we have markets and consumers who demand specialist products each designed to deliver optimum performance for a particular use. Some examples of the required formulae to meet various consumer demands are shown in Table 1.

Having built the oil blend with the required stability, melting and organoleptic properties, these blends then move to the next stage of formulation and processing before reaching the packing line.

Table 9.1   The principal characteristics required by consumers of different margarine, fats and oils formulation

Retail Products	*Consumer Requirement*
Hard packet margarine	Baking performance
	Price
Soft tub margarine	Spread performance
	Price
	Flavour
Nutritional margarine	All vegetable, good spread
	High in PUFA
	Flavour
Butter/vegetable blends	Low in SAFA,
	Flavour
	High in PUFA
Low fat spread	Good spreadability
	Low in calories
	Possibly all vegetable
Salad oil	All vegetable
	Clarity–good colour
	Low in SAFA
Solid vegetable oil	Frying fat
Solid margarines	Physical characteristics
	like butter

Commercial Products	
Long life frying oils	Maximum resistance to
	breakdown at frying
	temperature
	Good stability in food
Cake margarine	Good flavour and baking
	performance
	Excellent cake volume
High ratio shortening	Good baking performance
	Excellent cake volume and
	keeping quality
Puff pastry margarine	Toughness to handle in
	factory processing
	Good melt in mouth
Ice cream fats	Quick melt
	Good mouth feel
Cocoa butter equivalents	Compatibility with cocoa
	butter
	Good eating quality

Many of the product groupings require significantly different processing, but there are some common factors. Margarine-type products from whatever oils or fats require the formulation of a water phase—at its most simple 'brine'. All margarines and shortenings require freezing of some description to produce the crystal structure and plasticity the product requires. Minor ingredients need to be added such as flavours, emulsifiers, stabilisers, antioxidants.

Salad and cooking oils probably provide the best example of a product which needs minimal processing, after the final deodorisation. Apart from a final polish filtration, the product can go straight to the bottling line or delivery tank car. Minor ingredients which may be added are antioxidants or crystal inhibitors to prevent hazing and settling out, all of which, of course, must be declared on the label. The salad or cooking oil market is very much a commodity market of price brands with little or no speciality performance features demanded by the consumer. It is an area where there has to be particular attention paid to the stability and odour of the finished oil. Ultra violet light is a well known factor in the oxidation of oil, and life in a plastic bottle under supermarket lighting is quite demanding on the stability of an oil.

Other products in the fats and oil range all require crystallisation to some extent, and the crystallisation patterns of the various fats have an important part to play in the delivery of the required finished product performance. The freezing process has been the subject of considerable and continued development since the early days of margarine.

Initially, margarine was churned on butter equipment, but around 1905, the significant development was the new cooling drum or chill roll. This was a drum of 5–6 ft. diameter on which a thin layer of margarine emulsion was spread. The emulsion is made up by blending the oil phase and the brine phase in the correct proportions with agitation. Nowadays, with modern metering pumps this can be done continuously with extreme accuracy. Inside the drum, the coolant, which was brine or ammonia, was circulated to lower the temperature of the drum surface. This solidified the margarine emulsion on the outside of the drum, as it rotated, and after rotation through about 270° the solidified flake was scraped off, by a knife blade, into a waiting trolley. The flake was 'rested' to allow crystallisation to complete, before being compacted and extruded into blocks for packing.

Some cooling drums are still in use, particularly for products, such as puff pastry margarines, where crystal structure is vitally important, to provide the laminating properties necessary. By and large, however, this slow and labour intensive process has been replaced with successive developments which have made the process more efficient and hygienic through developments in freezing and crystallising on a continuous basis. Equipment companies such as Girdler, Schroder, Votator and Gerstenberg, have been involved in the development of their processes for many years and have now reached the position where margarine can be packed and boxed within a couple of minutes, all in an enclosed totally hygienic system. This is an enormous improvement over the earlier equipment, in which emulsion was made up before freezing, and the flake held in trolleys for several hours to allow the desirable crystal form to develop.

The modern process can be varied to suit almost any type of fat product from tub margarine, baker's shortening, to puff pastry margarine. Most importantly this stage of processing is key to controlling the crystal structure and rheology of the finished product. Rheology is a parameter that is often underrated in its importance in delivering the finished product characteristics. Following blending, the blend passes into the freezing unit (essentially a scraped surface heat exchanger in which the product is continually cooled on the internal surface and scraped off by circulating blades). Following this shock cooling to initiate crystallisation, the product passes to a 'B unit', generally uncooled, in which the product is worked vigorously by a series of rotating rods, sometimes called a 'picker box'. The number of tubes used and the degree of cooling and or working can be varied to suit the product being made, but, generally speaking, the product passes immediately from the picker box to the packing machine.

For some types of product, a final step, which is still part of the process of getting the desirable crystal structure, is to temper the packed product. This involves holding the product at about 80°F for up to 24 hours to stabilise the crystal form. This is particularly important for products which need to maintain plasticity over a wide temperature range and to hold that plasticity even when exposed to moderate extremes of temperature. For example, in the design of products for use in cake manufacturing, it is important that the fat should be in the desired range of consistency. Tempering the fat imparts a 'memory' which helps ensure that no matter what tempering cycle the fat has been through since manufacture, it will be of the right consistency when returned to 60°F before use in the bakery.

In summary, the processes used by the manufacturer of oils and fat products are; purification by neutralisation, bleaching and deodorisation; adjustment of actual triglyceride molecules, by either the chemical means of hydrogenation, or inter–esterification or physically through fractionation techniques; blending of the various stocks available to give the desired melting or nutritional characteristics; and finally the crystallisation or plasticisation processes to give a finished product of the correct consistency and texture to meet the performance requirements of the customer. It is the finished performance of the product which governs, to a very large extent, how the product should be formulated. The finished product requirements of a table spread margarine, for example, are very different from a puff pastry margarine or a product designed for the industrial frying of potato crisps.

Performance parameters to be considered for the table margarine could be summarised:

(1) Nutritional requirements.
(2) Spreading performance.
(3) Melting in the mouth.
(4) Flavour delivery.
(5) Shelf life.

Depending on the type and price of margarine, the importance of these features would probably appear in different orders of priority. For puff pastry margarine for the food manufacturer, important parameters could be:

(1) Ability to withstand vigorous working in the manufacturing process.
(2) Excellent tough laminating rheology.
(3) Nutritional requirement.

(4) Labelling requirement—no additives.
(5) Oil stability in the emulsion and also in extended shelf life of finished product.
(6) Excellent height in finished pastry.
(7) Sharp melt in the mouth for finished pastry.

Another example is the heavy duty frying oil, probably the most demanding use of any edible oil product:

(1) Resistance of chemical breakdown such as oxidation, polymerisation, or hydrolysis at temperatures up to 180°C.
(2) Should not go dark so as to discolour food.
(3) Pourable, pumpable at ambient temperature.
(4) Nutritional characteristics.
(5) Oil stability not only at the high temperature of the frying process, but also during the prolonged life of the potato crisp when this oil is exposed to air on the large surface area of the crisps.

These three examples help to explain why product formulations need to provide quite different base oil characteristics to meet the requirements of the finished product in order to meet the need to the final consumer.

FUTURE DEVELOPMENTS

The history of oils and fats processing, as has been indicated, has been one of constant change since the first products were made over a hundred years ago. Many of our older industries have suffered from the lack of development effort and progress stagnates. This has not been the case with the oils and fats industry and there are no signs of it happening today. Indeed, the new demands of the consumer are becoming greater, not only from the point of view of finished product performance, but nutritional requirements are becoming more important, and no doubt this trend will continue. Consumer awareness of the importance of the make-up of food is increasing, and, as in the past, the oils and fats industry will be making the necessary changes, to meet consumer demand. As an example, the current consumer dislike of additives, whether it is real, or stimulated by media publicity, is leading to the elimination of many additives that have been approved and widely used for years.

The antioxidant additive which many food manufacturers used to specify for their oil and fat product is disappearing, and oil processors are looking for long term oxidative stability through more thorough processing. Pesticide residues can now be detected analytically at very low levels, and, although it is known that processing reduces the levels of these chemicals, we will be looking for ways to reduce them still further. Alongside this, I have no doubt that there is also need to look at the other side of the coin to achieve lower usage of pesticides, and perhaps, achieve the same effect with safer compounds. In bakery fats, the move to vegetable formulae has been considerable in recent years, and many companies now prefer baking margarines without colour.

The development of low erucic acid rapeseed oil which has now virtually eliminated this fatty acid, was a triumph for the plant geneticist. I have no doubt that we will see many more developments of this type to give, for example, a less saturated palm oil.

The processes that are used to modify the characteristics of oils and fats are also changing, although many of the biochemical processes are not yet viable from an industrial viewpoint. Biochemistry and enzymatic processes can be used to modify triglycerides and the position of individual fatty acids on the triglyceride can be altered and controlled.

It is possible that the basic oils used in Europe will also change, and new processing techniques will be developed to meet these demands. We have been processing low erucic rapeseed oil grown in Europe for some 6–7 years and the learning curve has been very rapid. The benefit of Europe's first indigenous vegetable oil seed crop was not missed but there were some difficulties along the way. The second phase of rapeseed development 'the double low version' which also reduces the troublesome glucosinolate content of the meal, is promised to be in large scale production in the next few years.

Marine oil usage has been high in Europe for many years and should continue to provide a low cost alternative to vegetable oil. Perhaps also the content of polyunsaturated fatty acids of C20 and C22 chains will also give the oil a nutritional benefit over some vegetable oils, but it would seem difficult to achieve the basic stability necessary with such highly unsaturated fatty acids. At the same time, to hit them with the hydrogenation sledgehammer before including them in margarines, certainly does not make nutritional sense.

Taken together, these developments and processes enable the industry to provide good stability products of appropriate flavour and lubricity, both necessary parts of food acceptance in the judgement of the consumer. Many food products need an adequate level of fat or oil both to carry the flavour and also to improve the eating quality of the product. In many cases low fat products simply do not taste good.

Unfortunately, or fortunately to some including our own previous generations, they are calorie dense. This has been recognised and low calorie margarine has been developed together with high PUFA margarine and a general menu to meet consumer demand and indeed the COMA recommendation for fewer fat calories and particularly lower levels of saturated fatty acids. Future developments will enable us to continue to meet these requirements.

The pattern of change in the oil processing industry has been regular and progressive, driven by a need to meet consumer demands. This will continue, possibly at a greater pace. The industry has been dogged by restrictive legislation since its inception and, probably more in the US than in Europe, was the subject of much protectionist legislation. Despite this, it has survived and grown, and is today a major part of the food industry. Even today, we are now threatened by a punitive EEC Oils and Fats tax which seems to me to be totally the wrong way to make EEC farmers and the dairy industry efficient, and can only lead to more expensive margarine for the housewife.

I know I can speak for my own company and I suspect the same can be said for all the major companies which make up the European industry, when I say that we expect to be able to continue to design products to meet consumer need. Also, as in the past, we will continue to be guided in our formulation policies by the results of meaningful medical research in helping to provide safe and nutritional products. We value the British Nutrition Foundation in helping to provide a forum for the interchange of such information.

Although it is beyond the scope of this paper, no review of future developments would be complete that did not mention the development by Procter and Gamble of the zero-calorie fat substitute provisionally called Olestra, but also known as Sucrose Polyester. This has been the subject of a great deal of comment and consumer interest on both sides of the Atlantic. Essentially, the development uses the chemistry of a sucrose molecule substituted with the same fatty acids that occur in triglycerides. Olestra exhibits very similar properties to a triglyceride in that it tastes and performs like a fat or oil, and can be used to make a variety of products such as margarines, shortenings and frying oil. The big difference is that Olestra is an octaester and consequently is not digested by the body. It therefore contributes no calories to the diet, since it passes through the body without being absorbed. An application for approval in the US has been submitted to the FDA based on more than 20 years of research, encompassing more than 100 animal and human studies, confirming Olestra's safety and acceptability as a zero calorie fat and oil replacement. The development of Olestra therefore represents a major breakthrough and offers the prospect of food products which will meet the consumer demand for excellent taste and eating qualities whilst also meeting the medical recommendations to lower fat consumption, and provide a healthier range of finished goods.

10
Milk and milk products
F. HARDING

This overview of the dairy industry provides a brief perspective on developments in milk production and processing, and explains some of the changes in distribution and retailing. It also discusses the role of milk and milk products in the diet and looks at future developments in technology.

The dairy industry is the largest single sector of the UK food and drinks industry. Dairy products account for about 16% of UK consumer expenditure on food and over 50% of the beef consumed in the UK is derived from dairy herds. The annual value of milk produced by UK farmers is about £2 billion and the retail value of products made from it is about £4.5 billion.

Traditionally, the UK has been a net importer of dairy products. However, urged on by calls for food from our own resources, the industry increased production by about 2% per year until, in 1984, quotas were imposed on all EEC countries. No one can deny the logic of reducing milk production in the light of the storage costs created by the current Common Agricultural Policy. However, it would have been preferable to have seen demand stimulated by price reductions, allowing the natural law of supply and demand to operate. However, the decision to impose quotas was taken, and the UK, like other countries in the EEC, suffered a reduction in production. The impact on the UK has been particularly hard in that we currently produce *less* milk than our domestic require-ment. With the further cuts in quotas we will become even further dependent on imports and it can be estimated that we will only be able to supply the equivalent of 85% of our needs from home production. About 25% of our needs are, in fact, imported because UK products find their way to EEC storage. Contrast this with Holland who produce more than 3 times their domestic requirement and have a healthy export trade.

Currently the UK dairy industry and, indeed, the dairy industry worldwide, is going through difficult political and economic times. Ironically, one of the reasons for the present over-production of milk is the record of efficiency improvement in dairying. The dairy industry is therefore to some extent a victim of its own success.

DEVELOPMENTS IN MILK PRODUCTION

Improved breeding methods using genetic selection and artificial insemi-nation have led to a dramatic improvement in the yield and quality of milk per cow. The yield per cow is about 40% higher now than it was in 1969.

Another avenue of development involves one of the hormones that stimulate milk production, bovine somatotropin, which has been known for many years. Now scientists are able to produce bovine somatotropin by genetic manipulation of bacteria. Injection of cows with this naturally occurring, and perfectly safe, milk stimulant can give immediate increase in milk yield of about 20% per cow. This has an appreciable potential consumer impact, but it is also a clear example of the dramatic effect modern technology can have on an industry.

Modern technology has already dramatically changed the methods of milk production. In modern milking plants cows are automatically identified for computerised feeding in order to maximise the yield of milk per cow. Cows are machine milked and milk is transferred by pipeline into refrigerated farm vats where it is rapidly cooled to <5°C. It is normally collected each day and delivered to the processing dairy in insulated bulk vehicles. This can be contrasted with the days when town cows were kept and hand milked to provide town milk and milk was sold from open carts.

Changes in milk handling have dramatically improved the quality of milk and together with wider application of heat treatment by pasteurisation have effectively eliminated the risk of milkborne diseases. Untreated milk can still be a source of pathogens such as salmonella, originating largely from diseases of the cow. However, improved animal husbandry, together with pasteurisation (which effectively kills all pathogens) has led to an extremely good safety record with respect to milkborne diseases.

MILK QUALITY

The combined effects of refrigerated on-farm storage of milk, and the use of automated, computerised central testing laboratories, used for quality payment purposes, have significantly improved the quality of milk from farms. The bacteriological quality of the national milk supply improved 6–fold since centralised quality payment testing was introduced in 1982.

The incidence of antibiotics in milk arising from their use to control mastitis in the cow, also showed a 5–fold reduction over the past six years, and our quality control has reduced levels 40–fold since the 1960s when testing started. Milk is also surveyed for the presence of possible contaminants such as toxic trace metals (lead, cadmium, mercury), pesticides and aflatoxins and, of course, radionuclides, the levels of which, judged by modern highly sensitive analytical techniques, are extremely low.

PROCESSING OF LIQUID MILK

Whilst untreated milk is still sought after by those who either value the flavour or are unable to obtain heat treated milk, most milk (85%) consumed in the UK is pasteurised with a small proportion (8%) being sterilised or UHT (ultra high temperature) treated. Louis Pasteur in the early 1860s was the first to study the science behind the preservation value of moderate heating of liquid. Different combinations of time/temperature conditions have been used with milk with the high temperature short time (HTST) continuous flow pasteuriser, heating milk to 161°F for 15 sec being the most commonly used combination. Pasteurisation kills any pathogens which are likely to be of public health concern and also kills milk-souring organisms, thus extending the shelf life. Careful plant control is necessary in order to ensure that adequate pasteurisation time/temperature conditions are achieved and that there is no recontamination of heated milk by raw milk. The native enzyme phosphatase is destroyed at normal pasteurisation temperatures and is used as an 'end product' test as an assurance of correct plant operation. Pasteurisation does not kill all bacteria in milk but those which survive, the thermoduric bacteria, tend not to grow at the low temperatures at which pasteurised products are stored.

The shelf life of pasteurised milk depends on the level of post heat-treatment contamination, the storage temperature of the final product and, to some extent, on the bacterial load of the raw milk used. A shelf life of 3–9 days is normally sufficient for bottled milk delivered daily to the home, where temperature control down the chain is difficult to maintain. Increased sales of cartonned pasteurised milk through supermarkets has led to demands for a longer shelf life of ten days or more. However, cartonned milk, aseptically packaged after pasteurisation, and kept at low temperatures (4–5°C), can have a shelf life of 21–28 days.

The two major changes occurring in liquid milk buying patterns, have been a move from doorstep delivery towards shop sales, which now account for 23% of total sales, and the diversification of the type of milk consumed. There has been a rapid increase in the consumption of low fat milks (skimmed or semi-skimmed milk) and together these now account for about 21% of total milk consumed compared with about 5% in 1983/84. Interest is also currently being shown in hydrolysed milk for the lactose intolerant (in which lactose has been converted into glucose) and in calcium-enriched milk. Breakfast Milk and Cereal Time are two competing, higher fat milks, produced to satisfy a specific breakfast opportunity.

The active Research and Development Unit in the Milk Marketing Board has the objective of increasing the consumption of added value products. One of our areas of research interest, is in the extension of milk-based drinks, particularly in areas that will compete with the lucrative soft drink market. In one such development we have repackaged milk in plastic cans, with a ring pull aluminium top, suitable for easy outdoor consumption. The time/temperature heat treatment of the milk has been modified to give a shelf life of about 10 weeks, with minimum flavour damage to the product.

Flavoured milk drinks also have a niche in the market and we are extending the range of flavours available (e.g. Mars drinks). Carbonated milk and whey based drinks and products such as drinking yogurt and kefir are also being researched.

The success of Baileys Cream Liqueur has led to many other products being produced. This is a product where one is loath to make positive nutritional claims, it is one of self-indulgence, yet it is very popular, selling 700 000 cases a year in the UK. Lighter alcoholic milk with flavouring and egg nogs are also being researched. The drink market has a massive market income (£2.3 billion) and much work is being undertaken to broaden the consumption patterns of milk from simply an additive to tea.

MILK PRODUCTS

Cheese

The majority of milk produced is consumed as liquid milk, butter or cheese. Within the UK we are high in the league table with respect to liquid milk consumption yet relatively low in terms of cheese consumption. It has been recognised for many thousands of years that cheese is a very good way of preserving most of the nutrionally rich components in milk. Variations in the manufacturing conditions, for example, amount of fat, degree of pressing of the cheese, amount of salt added, maturation time and conditions, has led to the production of many thousands of cheese varieties around the world. Traditionally, in the UK we are used to hard, pressed cheese such as Cheddar and other regional varieties such as Cheshire, Caerphilly, Lancashire and the only UK cheese which has its name protected by the *Appelation Controlée* Regulation – Stilton.

Many believe that our limited cheese consumption statistics would be improved if we followed the Continental practice and ate our cheese *before* our palates have been dulled and our appetites satisfied by a heavy dessert. We are trying to expand the consumption of cheese by means of new product development. Restoration of old cheese varieties such as Blue Vinney, the production of home produced 'foreign' cheeses such as Feta or Camembert, (there is, for example, a very successful Somerset Brie) and new varieties such as Lymeswold, are all aimed at stimulating interest in cheese consumption. The greater interest in foreign travel has altered tastes and eating habits and cheese consumption is a part of this.

Cheesemaking has not changed dramatically over the years. However, there are areas of technological development. Ultrafiltration, a means of concentrating the protein and lactose in milk, is now being practised as a means of 'dewatering' milk prior to cheesemaking. This has economic benefits and can lead to increased yields. Starter control has been improved, through the use of genetically engineered bacteria, leading to improved flavour and greater quality consistency of production. Genetic engineering has also been used in the production of natural enzymes which are responsible for the production of the flavours in matured Cheddar cheese and recent experiments have shown that maturation and storage times can be reduced by 50% with the production of a high grade cheese by the addition of these enzymes to Cheddar cheese.

Butter

Butter, like margarine, must, by law, contain a minimum of 80% fat. It is a product which has been losing its market share over recent years, as has margarine. The development has been in the area of spreads. Dairy spreads, blending butter and hydrogenated vegetable oils, and low fat spreads, both dairy and non-dairy, have been taking an increasing share in this market. A possible development is the production of a more spreadable butter by significantly decreasing the hard saturated fat and by increasing the level of softer mono-unsaturated fatty acids in milk, This can be achieved by altering the cow's feed.

Other dairy products

Since EEC quota restrictions place a limit on the volume of milk which can be produced, it is important to dairy farmers that the market for their milk is the most profitable. Milk sold for different end uses brings different returns. The use of milk constituents as ingredients in the food industry (high grade whey proteins in bakery, high melting point fat fractions in the baking business, hyrolysed lactose as a sweetener) are all being explored.

There is also considerable interest in new products. The market is segmented. There is a growth of interest in low fat milks, cheeses, yogurts etc. There is also an interest in high fat 'luxury' products, dairy desserts, real dairy ice cream and high fat yogurts as well as products such as Channel Island Breakfast Milk.

The dairy industry has to be aware of consumer needs and to continue to provide the products the consumer wants. Product developments are expanding in range to do just this.

TECHNOLOGICAL THREATS AND OPPORTUNITIES

Three of the many areas of technological development are, genetically manipulated bacteria in cultured products; the milk production stimulant bovine somatotropin—currently on trial for administration to the cow to increase milk yield; and added enzymes, produced form genetic manipulation of bacteria, used to accelerate the maturation of cheese. These all offer significant opportunities—but they also provide a threat.

The consumer perceives milk and dairy products to be 'natural'—this image is tarnished by the thought that scientists have 'mucked about' with the product. These developments are similar to the process of irradiation. The food industry need to develop a better public awareness of new technological opportunities.

NUTRITIONAL ASPECTS

The role of the dairy industry in nutrition is another area, where, sadly, the consumers have been left with misunderstandings. Milk and dairy products are virtually free from additives and have for thousands of years made a significant contribution to the human diet. It was therefore something of a shock for the industry to suffer the stark attacks it faced from dietary zealots intent on reducing saturated fat consumption. Articles in the popular press did not call for the balanced reduction in fat requested by the COMA report, more in vogue were headlines such as 'Killer Cow' and 'Butter causes epidemic of coronary heart disease' Such misleading interpretations of the COMA Report and extreme diets aimed at rapid weight reduction could, clearly, lead to unhealthy dietary changes. Milk and dairy products supply two thirds of our dietary calcium in a highly bioavailable form. Dairy products are also a good source of a large number of valuable trace elements and vitamins and an inexpensive source of protein and energy, the latter being important for the young as well as growing and active adults. It is wrong to avoid any single food sources such as dairy products since this might bring problems of dietary deficiencies, for example, in mineral balance.

Part of the case for dairy products is that they complement other foods (milk and cereal, bread and butter), hence making high fibre foods, for example, more palatable and possibly enhancing the bioavailability of trace elements in the mixture. Our knowledge of human nutrition and its impact on health is in its infancy. There is a need to maintain a cautious, balanced approach to the effect of diet and health, avoiding the sort of overreaction we have seen in recent years, if the consumer is to be helped, rather than thoroughly confused by developing knowledge.

11
Influence of modern methods of production and processing on the nutritional value of potatoes and potato products

J. C. HUGHES AND R. M. FAULKS

INTRODUCTION

Despite the popularity and convenience of rice and pasta, the annual *per capita* consumption of potatoes has fluctuated around 100kg for the last two decades apart from a significant drop in 1975 and 1976 due to shortages resulting from very hot dry summers. Since 1976 consumption has continued to rise and has been over 100kg for the last 4 or 5 years (Figure 1). However, the greatest change has not been in the amount consumed but in the form in which it is eaten i.e. whether it be fresh or processed. In the last 20 years consumption of processed potato has risen steadily (apart from the peaks in 1975 and 1976 when large amounts of dehydrated potato were imported to cope with shortages) from around 8% in 1966 to around 28% today (Figure 2).

Compositionally the potato is an exceptional vegetable, it contains about 20% dry matter which is mainly starch, with small amounts of sugar, protein, cell wall and ash. Because of the quantity consumed, it makes a

173

significant nutritional contribution to the intake of some nutrients, e.g. carbohydrates (including dietary fibre), protein, ascorbic acid, thiamin and iron (Table 1). In addition to its nutritional content, the potato, in common with many food plants, contains substances which are toxic if eaten in sufficient quantities, but when eaten in normal amounts are harmless. The potato contains a number of steroid compounds of which

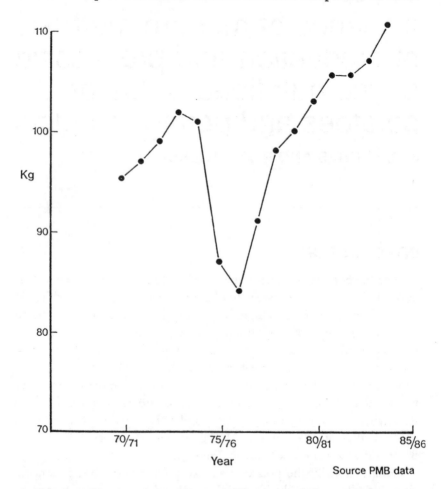

Figure 11.1   Potatoes moving into human consumption in UK *(Scource: PMB data)*

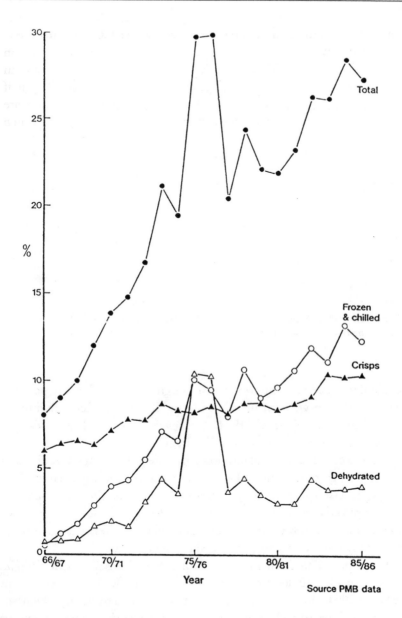

Figure 11.2   % moving into human consumption as processed products
(Scource: PMB data)

Table 11.1 Contribution of fresh potatoes to total dietary intake of some nutrients

	Contribution (% of total intake)	Relative ranking of potatoes as dietary source
Carbohydrate	12.3	3
Energy	6.1	4
Protein	4.5	6
Ascorbic acid	30.0	1
Thiamin	11.9	2
Iron	6.8	3
Dietary fibre	17.7	1

(Source: Finglas and Faulks, 1985, from MAFF National Food Survey, 1979 and Food Composition Tables, 1978)

α-solanine is the most important. Although in normal healthy potatoes the amounts are well within what is considered to be the safe limit of 20mg/100g (Parnell *et al.*,)1984, the levels of glycoalkaloids can be influenced by variety, growing and storage.

Because of the nutritional importance of the potato to the UK diet, and the increasing consumption of processed potatoes, the argument of fresh versus processed is of some significance. At the same time, it should not be overlooked that during the last few decades considerable changes have occurred in methods of production. The effects of these changes on the nutritional value of potatoes also need to be considered.

The impact of these changes in production methods is evident from the fact that yields doubled from around 20 to about 40 tonnes per hectare between 1954 and 1984. Higher yields have resulted from improvements in varieties, improved seed health and husbandry (higher inputs of fertilizers and the use of pesticides and fungicides). Since up to about 70%

of the potato maincrop is stored for some time the impact of changes in storage is also very relevant.

This review will concentrate primarily, on the influence of variety, husbandry, storage, cooking and processing on the nutritional value – in the broadest sense – of the potato.

VARIETY, HARVESTING AND STORAGE CONDITIONS

Variety

As in the case of other food crops, there has been a dramatic change in potato varieties grown in the UK in the last 20 years (Figure 3). For example, in 1968 about 50% of the maincrop consisted of 2 varieties bred

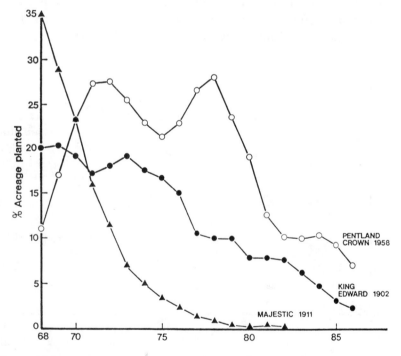

Figure 11.3   % acreage of maincrop varieties 1968–1985 *(Scource:PMB data)*

early this century–Majestic and King Edward, and it is mainly on these varieties that earlier Food Composition Tables are based. Today these varieties have largely disappeared and in their place there are a number of other varieties, all competing against one another (Figure 4). Two of these, Maris Piper and Desiree, are mainly sold for domestic use, whilst the other two shown, Record and Pentland Dell, are primarily grown for processing.

Considerable changes have also taken place in the husbandry of the potato crop since the late 1960s. The rate of application of fertiliser has steadily increased (Table 2) while in drier areas irrigation is now used to improve yields. More general use of improved pest and disease control agents is also being practised on the growing crop. Today most maincrop potatoes are harvested mechanically, whereas 20 years ago hand picking was common, a practice that is now almost exclusive to 'new potatoes'. The increase in mechanisation for harvesting, grading and moving into and out of stores has dramatically increased the levels of mechanical injury

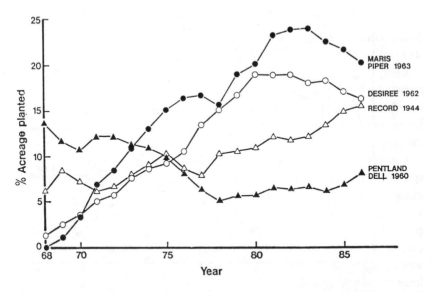

Figure 11.4   % acreage of maincrop varieties 1968–1985 *(Scource: PMB data)*

Table 11.2   Changes in rate of application of fertiliser to maincrop potatoes. (Kg per hectare)

Year	N	P	K
1969	164	175	249
1973	176	189	244
1977	181	186	251
1981	199	197	266
1984	216	230	281

P as P_2O_5, K as K_2O

(Source: Rothamsted Experimental Station, Statistics Dept., Harpenden, Herts. AL5 2JO)

(cuts, scuffing and internal bruising) and consequently greater losses in store and during preparation.

Over 20 years ago about 50% of potatoes were stored indoors, the remainder being stored in clamps outside. Today almost all stored potatoes are kept in purpose built stores or barns and 50% of these, mainly those intended to be kept for more than three months are treated with chemical agents to control disease and sprout growth.

Control of sprout growth is essential during long term storage since sprouting can lead to the loss of quality and undesirable biochemical changes, particularly increases in the levels of reducing sugars which are a key factor in the colour and taste of fried products. This problem is of particular concern to potato processors and is currently being tackled by careful control of store temperatures and the use of sprout suppressants, while in the longer term efforts are being made to breed potatoes that have long dormancy or which do not accumulate reducing sugars over long periods in store.

Other changes include contract growing of potatoes for processing and pre-packing, where farmers may be advised on the optimal management of the crop, from the selection of the variety through to storage of the harvested potatoes.

NUTRITIONAL VALUE

The possible effect of changes in varieties and modern methods of production on the UK diet has been investigated at IFR Norwich Laboratory for MAFF (Finglas and Faulks, 1984). Over two seasons, four maincrop potato cultivars, together with early varieties, were purchased every 12 weeks from a range of retail outlets in three principal consumer areas (London, Birmingham and Glasgow) and analysed for a range of nutrients. Nutrients found to be lower than the values quoted in the Food Composition Tables (Paul and Southgate, 1978) were riboflavin and niacin (50%), potassium (40%), iron, copper and zinc (20–30%) whilst thiamin and total folate were 2–3 times higher. Total ascorbate was similar at harvest, but declined rapidly thereafter. Some of these differences may reflect improvement in analyses. However if we examine the relative ranking of these constituents in the current survey with those of the earlier date we see that they are in many cases very similar (Table 3).

No significant effect of variety, centre or season was found for starch, protein, dietary fibre or fat. However there was a significant affect of these factors, and storage, on vitamin C. The lower level of vitamin C possibly reflects change away from King Edward, a variety high in ascorbate. Nevertheless the potato is still the main source of vitamin C in the UK diet.

Finglas and Faulks concluded that, although composition differed from the earlier Food Composition Tables, it was unlikely that these changes would be of major nutritional significance except in those groups of the population that depend heavily on potatoes. Whilst the data provides a reassuring picture of the current situation, it will, however, need to be reassessed periodically as new commercial varieties are produced. The need to reassess the situation may be more important now than in the past, because of the increased use of wild species in breeding programmes to widen the genetic pool, in an endeavour to increase, for example, disease resistance, and improve processing and storage quality. The characteristics

Table 11.3 Comparison of two surveys of the nutritional value of potatoes

	Contribution (% of total intake)		Relative ranking of potatoes as dietary source	
	Earlier	*Recent*	*Earlier*	*Recent*
Carbohydrates				
Starch	21.0	17.0	2	2
Dietary Fibre	17.7	15.2	1	1
Carbohydrate	12.3	10.1	3	3
Energy	6.1	5.2	4	5
Fat	0.2	0.4	44	28
Protein				
(N x 6.25)	4.5	4.3	6	6
Minerals				
Copper	15.8	8.4	1	3
Iron	6.8	5.4	3	3
Zinc	5.0	4.3	6	6
Phosphorus	5.0	4.8	4	4
Calcium	1.3	—	10	—
Vitamins				
Vitamin C	30.0	28.0	1	1
Pyridoxine (B_6)	28.0	—	1	—
Folate	12.0	>12.0	2	—
Thiamin (B_1)	11.9	21.6	2	1
Pantothenate	11.0	—	2	—
Niacin	10.6	5.3	2	4
Riboflavin (B_2)	3.4	1.7	8	11

(Source: Finglas and Faulks, 1985)

of these species, their inheritance and expression, are largely unknown, particularly in relation to nutritional value.

A cautionary tale can be related about the importance of screening the progeny from such crosses with wild species in breeding programmes. In 1970 it was discovered that a new American variety 'Lenape', which had been bred for the processing industry, had very high levels of glycoalkaloids over a range of sites in Canada and the US (Akeley *et al.*, 1968, Zitnak and Johnston, 1970). The high levels of glycoalkaoids were attributed to its ancestry which included an unusal wild species *Solanum chacoense*. The variety was immediately withdrawn from commerce in 1970. Varieties coming into trial in the UK are now screened for glycoalkaloids and have to have levels less than 20mg/100g. Since glycoalkaloid content is known to be affected by conditions during growth, storage and handling as well as variety, a survey was carried out to assess the levels of glycoalkaloids reaching the consumer through fresh and processed products from 6 collection areas in the UK (Davies and Blincow, 1984). Only 2 samples, out of the 133 analysed, had levels above 20mg/100g, and these were in 2 samples of early varieties where consideration of continuing the monitoring is necessary.

We can therefore conclude, on the evidence of these two surveys carried out at Norwich for MAFF, that modern methods of production and storage have not had a marked effect on the nutritional value or safety of the potatoes reaching our table. The situation is also reassuring with breeding material and varieties currently in the pipeline. A survey of the nutritional value of such material in trial at the National Institute of Agricultural Botany, Cambridge, and the Plant Breeding Institute Cambridge, showed that this material was not substantially different from current varieties (Faulks, unpublished data). However, as a defensive position, there is a case for evaluating the nutritional content of new potato varieties at some stage during trialing, in addition to glycoalkaloid screening.

PROCESSING

Processed potato products form an important part of the UK diet and account for nearly 30% of the potatoes that we eat today. This is in marked contrast to the 8% that we ate 20 years ago. At that time our consumption of processed products was largely crisps, at 6%, with dehydrated potato and frozen chips contributing around 0.5%. Whilst the consumption of crisps has risen steadily during the last 20 years it less than doubled. However, the consumption of frozen chips has increased dramatically from a very low base level to overtake crisps at about 12%.

On the other hand consumption of dehydrated potatoes, in one form or another, has remained at around 5% over the last decade, except in 1975 and 1976, the years of shortage. The main use of dehydrated potato is in the non-domestic market, where it is increasingly being used for extruded snack products, where a high specification powder low in reducing sugars is required.

Processing differs from domestic cooking in that a consistent product with good storage characteristics has to be produced. This generally involves more preparative and heating stages than in the home, and consequently, potentially greater nutritional losses, and the use of processing aids and additives. Sulphite is used to prevent enzymic browning during the first stage of processing, the peeling, slicing and cutting of whole tubers, for chips and dehydration, but not for crisps. Concern is being expressed about the use of sulphite, not only because of its well known destructive effects on thiamin (B_1) but also because it has been implicated in triggering asthma attacks in some sensitive individuals. One possible solution to this problem is the use of alternative antioxidants or, in the longer term, to breed improved varieties with low potential for browning. Collaborative work between Norwich and Birmingham University, to identify and characterise the genetic basis of low browing in potatoes, is being carried out using the wild species *S. Hjertingii*.

Blanching and cooking of potato pieces in water or steam leads to losses of thermally labile nutrients and to leaching. Most vulnerable are vitamin C and the monovalent cations, especially potassium. In the case of dehydrated potato there is an additional effect of the long period of cyclical drying during the 'add back' process which further increases labile nutrient losses. During frying, baking or microwave cooking there are no leaching losses but some water soluble components may migrate to the surface of the cooked tissue. Since the majority of processed potatoes are fried, or intended for frying, uptake of cooking oils and fats is a major factor, not only because of the cost, but because of increased awareness of the health implications of fat consumption by the consumer. In addition to process variables, tuber composition, particularly dry matter, influences fat uptake.

Processed products also differ from fresh in that in order to extend their shelf life some method of preservation must be used. For the bulk of processed potato, freezing is the method of choice, whereas dry products e.g. crisps or granules, may simply be stored under cool, dry conditions. However, deterioration may still occur, causing losses of vitamins and oxidative deterioration of fats and oils. For this reason, preservatives and antioxidants may be used, although their use is now minimal in crisps and frozen french fries, quality being maintained by improved distribution and marketing.

Nutritional considerations

On the face of it, the common perception is that processed foods are nutritionally inferior to the 'real' thing. However this view loses sight of the fact that, both in the domestic and catering preparation of potatoes, losses of nutrients inevitably occur, and the extent to which this happens will depend on the type of cooking and the extent of warm holding prior to service. As is well recognised, the commercial production of processed potato products adversely affects some of the nutrients, but manufacturers take nutritional value seriously (sales promotion) and keep processing, and hence losses, to a minimum (economics).

Additionally, any nutritional comment should take into consideration other advantages of access to processed products e.g. minimal preparation, convenience, individual food choice and availability. From a nutritional standpoint, it would appear to be better to have a processed potato product, even if it does have a reduced micronutrient content, than to have nothing, or a substitute of lower nutritional value. Strict comparisons between the vitamin content of, say, french fries produced from fresh potatoes and frozen french fries are therefore only valid if the consumer makes the substitution of one for the other.

Nutritional data are valuable in assessing the nutritional quality of the diet as a whole, as well as providing information on the dietary role of potatoes and potato products.

The Laboratory of the Government Chemist has recently carried out a survey of the nutritional value of a range of processed potato products for MAFF, and some of the data is presented in Tables 4 and 5, with the comparative data for the same product from fresh potatoes. Total ascorbate and thiamin data are presented in Table 4. These nutrients are key ones because the potato is the major source of vitamin C in the diet, which is easily destroyed by heat and atmospheric oxidation during preparation

Table 11.4   Total ascorbate and thiamin content of processed and non-processed potato products. (mg/100g, as consumed)

	Total Ascorbate mg	Thiamin mg
Crisps		
Traditional	45	0.11[a]
	17	0.19[b]
Chips		
Processed		
Oven Ready	8 – 12	0.11 – 0.12[a]
Frozen	12 – 16	0.16[a]
	4	0.09[b]
Non-processed		
Old potatoes	6 – 14	0.20[c]
	5 – 16	0.10[b]
New Potatoes	13	0.20[c]
Mash		
Instant mash	26	0.01[c]
Fresh mash	4 – 12	0.08[c]
Boiled		
Old potato	4 – 9	0.20[c]
New potato	9	0.10[b]

[a] MAFF unpublished data   [b] Composition of Foods, 1978
[c] Finglas and Faulks 1984.

and processing, and because thiamin is destroyed by sulphite, commonly used to prevent enzymic browning.

From the data in Table 4 it can be seen that the total ascorbate levels in processed and non-processed chips are comparable, whereas crisps and instant mash have more. In the case of crisps, the short fry time, and the concentrating effect of moisture loss, result in a total ascorbate value between two and four times that in fresh potato. In instant mash, the ascorbate is present as an ascorbic acid ester, added to fortify the product and to act as an antioxidant, since most of the natural ascorbate has been destroyed.

Thiamin levels, in most cases, are between 0.1–0.2mg/100g. However substantial losses are seen in instant mashed potato and in crisps where the losses are offset by increases in dry matter. These losses may arise either because of the use of sulphite or because of the thermal processing. Other vitamins are likely to suffer lower losses than vitamin C.

Most other nutrients, e.g. sugars, starch, dietary fibre, protein and minerals, are relatively unaffected by processing, unless leaching is employed in the process to reduce the sugar content. In this case some losses of amino acids and the more soluble minerals (e.g. potassium) will occur.

Thus the production of food items from potato, either domestically or through commercial processing, alters the nutritional value, not only by reducing the amount of micronutrients, by comparison with the raw value, but frequently also by increasing the nutritional value, especially energy density, by increasing the dry matter and by addition of fats and oils.

Of the potato consumed, most of the processed (30% of total consumption) picks up fat during processing or preparation. Of the remaining 70% at least half is eaten fried as chips or roast or with fat added in either mashed or baked. From a nutritional point of view, excess consumption of fat is implicated in a number of disease states, and recommendations have been made to encourage a reduction in fat in most people's diets. The fat content of both processed and domestically produced potato products (Table 5) is therefore of interest, and this is reflected in attempts to reduce the fat content of processed products. The fat content of crisps is around 30–35%, and because of this they have been criticised, especially since they are commonly consumed by children as a snack food. A substantial reduction in fat content is possible as seen from the data for low fat crisps. Whether low fat crisps become the norm will depend on consumer acceptability and the economics of their production.

The range of fat content of frozen chips, when prepared for consumption, is only marginally higher than the domestic product, and this may be because they are fried twice. An alternative explanation may be that frozen chips are smaller and hence have a greater surface area per unit mass through which fat absorbtion can occur. Oven chips, however, have a lower fat content than their domestic counterparts. The slightly higher value for fat in chips from new potatoes probably results from excessive frying times used to achieve a satisfactory colour, since the reducing sugar levels in this type of potato are generally low.

Recent trends in the diversification of processed potato products include potato waffles, hash browns, baked potatoes and other specialist products. Nutritionally these changes are welcome since they offer the

Table 11.5 Fat content of crisps and chips (g/100g. as consumed)

	Fat (g)	Reference
Crisps		
Low fat	25 – 26	Pack declaration
Traditional	33.6	MAFF unpublished
	35.9	Food Tables, 1978
Chips		
Processed		
Oven-ready	4.2–4.4	MAFF unpublished
	4.8–5.6	Prince, 1986
Frozen	10.2–16.7	MAFF unpublished
	18.9	Food tables, 1978
Non-processed		
Old potatoes	6.0–8.0	Finglas and Faulks, 1984
	6.2–11.0	Prince, 1986
	7.0–15.0	Food Tables, 1978
New potatoes	12.1	Finglas and Faulks, 1984

scope not only to improve the nutritional quality of processed potato products but a wider choice to the consumer. Future trends in processed potato products will probably see these products taking an increasing share of the market whilst possibilities of producing novel potato products remain largely unexplored.

Acknowledgement

The authors gratefully acknowledge the Ministry of Agriculture, Fisheries and Food for their kind permission to use some of their unpublished data.

References

Akeley, R. W., and Mills, W. R., Cunningham, C. E. and Watts, J. (1968). Lenape: A new potato variety high in solids and chipping quality. *Am. Pot. J.*, 45, 142–5

Davies, A. M. C. and Blincow, P. J. (1984). The glycoalkaloid content of potatoes and potato products sold in the UK. *J. Sci. Food Agric.*, 35 553–7

Finglas, P. M. and Faulks, R. M. (1984). Nutritional composition of UK retail potatoes both raw and cooked. *J. Sci. Food Agric.* 35, 1347–6

Finglas, P. M. and Faulks, R. M. (1985). A new look at potatoes. *Nutr. Fd. Sci.*, Jan/Feb 12-14

Ministry of Agriculture, Fisheries and Food. (1979). *Household food consumption and expenditure*. Annual Report of the National Food Survey Committee, HMSO.

Parnell, A., Bhuva, V. S. and Bintcliffe, E. J. B. (1984). The glycoalkaloid content of potato varieties. *J. Natn. Inst. Agric. Bot.*, 16, 535–41

Paul, A. A. and Southgate, D. A. T. (1978). In McCance and Widdowson *The Composition of Foods*. (4th edn.) (HMSO)

Prince, D., King, T. and Postle, G. (1986). Fat in chips: How aware are the public and do they care. *Nutr. Fd. Sci.*, Sept/Oct. 4-5

Zitnak, A. and Johnston, G. R. (1970). Glycoalkaloid content of B5141-6 potatoes. *Am. Pot. J.*, 47, 256-60

Appendix:
Food processing —
a nutritional perspective

INTRODUCTION

The contribution made by processed food to the diet of the average individual is considerable. In 1985, for example, households in Britain spent £19 862 million on commercially processed food* out of a total £27 090 million spent on food for home consumption, that is approximately 73% (MAFF, 1986).

Most foods cannot be regarded as suitable for human consumption in their raw, unprocessed state. Some, such as cereal grains, only become readily digestible and palatable after substantial processing, while meat, fish and most vegetables require preparation and cooking before they can be eaten. Other raw foods contain toxic components which make processing essential to reduce or eliminate them (for example, the hae-magglutinins in many seed legumes or the trypsin inhibitors in raw soy beans). Furthermore, if foods are not suitably protected and preserved, they can act as substrates for microorganisms or food for insects, rodents and other animals. Such conditions, if they occur, always result in loss and often present a hazard to health. Processing, by virtue of its preservative

---

* *Processed foods are defined for the purposes of this paper as all food except fresh fish, slaughtered meat, vegetables, fruit and eggs.*

189

action, minimises loss and substantially contributes to the nutritional adequacy of the food supply. In addition, a number of foods are nutritionally enriched during processing (for example, flour used for bread making).

Almost all raw food materials, in the condition in which they are taken from the living plant or the slaughtered animal, change with time owing to chemical reactions between their components. It is a function of the food industry to provide suitable environments to allow raw foods to be transported around the globe, without detrimental changes taking place.

On arrival at their destination these foods may then be distributed for purchase and consumption or employed as raw materials for further processing. If their use in manufacture is to be deferred for a period of time, raw foods may require some form of preservation. The development of the food industry has vastly increased the availability (both seasonal and geographical) of traditional foodstuffs and introduced hitherto unknown foods into the UK food supply. Ready access to a variety of different foods, both raw and processed, from every part of the world and at all seasons is accepted as the norm by most consumers in the UK.

The present adequacy of virtually all UK diets, in terms of energy and essential nutrients, was only established in the period during and immediately after World War II. While this improvement depended upon an improved general standard of living, increased efficiency in farming and greater variety from an expanding food industry were essential.

THE GENERAL OBJECTIVES AND METHODS OF FOOD PROCESSING

The initial discovery and effective early use of the main agents employed in the processing and preservation of foods – heating and chilling, evaporating and drying, freezing, fermenting, preserving with acid, salt or sugar, grinding and mixing, emulsifying and foaming – arose largely from intelligent observation of natural and chance events. Contemporary scientific research has extended and modified many of these processes to give increased production, reduced wastage and better standards of hygiene, but there have been few fundamentally new physical, chemical or biological methods developed for food processing and preservation. Of those that are new techniques, two of the best known are food irradiation and microwave heating. Both depend on the action of radiation on matter, the understanding of which has only come in the 20th century.

Processing agents

Most food processing techniques use a combination of agents either together in one stage or independently in successive stages.

Physical agents

The majority of domestic or commercial methods of food processing are physical in nature — heat, cold, change of state (evaporation, distillation, drying, freezing), subdivision (cutting, chopping, crushing, milling, grinding), separation (sieving, centrifugation, filtration), mixing, emulsification, foaming and exposure to radiation. Most are used to transform raw foods into more acceptable forms for eating. Others have preservation of the foods as their sole or main purpose (for example, freezing, drying, and exposure to high energy radiation), while the remainder combine both objectives (for example, heating).

Whatever the process, the mode and intensity of the agent must be specified and controlled to ensure safety and to secure the desired result. Where preservation is the main objective, the intensity achieved must secure the required destruction of microorganisms, degree of inactivation of enzymes or reduction in chemical reaction rate as appropriate. (The effects of physical methods of food processing are dealt with in more detail elsewhere in this paper.)

Chemical agents

Preservation Preservation by chemical means is of ancient origin. Most bacteria grow readily in moist, temperate or warm environments that avoid extremes of acidity or alkalinity. The main food poisoning organisms in particular, need near neutral conditions for growth and multiplication. Foods that are naturally acid (for example, most fruits), foods that have acid added to them and foods in which acids are released by the action of harmless bacteria (for example, those introduced by the starter cultures used in the making of yogurt and cheese) are thereby given a valuable measure of preservation. Many fungi are more tolerant than bacteria of moderately acid conditions, so they require further control, perhaps by heating. Salt and sugar, by reducing the availability of water to microorganisms, act as preservatives against bacterial attack. Almost all spoilage bacteria cease to grow in concentrations of 15% salt or 60% sugar although some fungi can survive and multipy in higher concentrations.

Smoking The smoking of meat and fish is an ancient method of processing valued not only for its preservation action but also for the characteristic taste it imparts to its products. Smoking is often preceded by a curing treatment using brine and other curing salts.

The preservation action of smoking is two-fold. Hard woods such as oak, elm and ash produce a smoke, containing aldehydes, phenols and acids which have a bactericidal and antioxidant action. The process also imparts a surface dehydration to the foodstuff which gives an additional measure of preservation. The quality and quantity of smoke, rate of heat transfer, humidity, and circulation of gas are usually tightly controlled. Some loss of the more heat-labile vitamins can occur (notably thiamin), but these losses are not usually considered nutritionally significant.

There are a number of other preservatives that may be used. These include sulphur dioxide, benzoic acid, sodium nitrite and nitrate, sodium and potassium sulphite, and propionic, lactic and sorbic acids, all of which are selected according to the preservation action required. The list of chemical preservatives and often their mode of use is controlled by regulation and their safety is reviewed periodically.

Food Additives Preservatives form part of a larger group of substances known as food additives. The food additives permitted by law serve a wide variety of functions. They may prevent or delay oxidation and rancidity, assist in stabilising emulsions and foams, adjust acidity or alkalinity, give colour or flavour, or act as a solvent. Additives are divided into categories depending on their function, and almost all are controlled by restriction to a permitted list. Flavours are not regulated in this way. There are many flavours in use, some are synthetic but many derive from natural sources.

In 1976 the Food Additives and Contaminants Committee recommended that; despite many difficulties, flavours should also be controlled by a permitted list system; the EEC is currently involved in efforts to implement this recommendation. Additives must be named in the list of ingredients with their category name (for example, preservative) plus either their specific chemical name or their serial number (if any) or both. When the additive is also permitted throughout the EEC, the serial number is prefixed by the letter 'E'.

Modification Chemical agents may be used to achieve specific and desirable modifications of foodstuffs. A good example of this is the hydrogenation of oils.

Hydrogenation Most commonly, the conversion of a liquid, unsaturated oil into a more solid, saturated form is achieved by hydrogenation. The oil is heated in the presence of a catalyst (usually nickel) and hydrogen gas is bubbled in under pressure. The hydrogen combines with the constituent unsaturated fatty acids in the oil. By careful choice of catalyst and temperature, the oil can be selectively hydrogenated so as to achieve a product with precisely the degree of unsaturation and hence physical and chemical characteristics that are desired. The overall result is a 'hardening' of the oil to give physical, nutritional and keeping properties which are more like those of a saturated fat. This process is used widely in the manufacture of margarines.

Biological agents

The remaining group of agents is that of microorganisms. These, in the course of their growth, can modify the food in which they are growing to transform it to give a new and different product. It is also possible for a microorganism to use up the food supplied to it and itself become the new raw material.

Modification and transformation The acid producing action of selected bacteria, added as a starter culture to mixtures of milk and skimmed milk is the key step in making yogurt. A similar acid production, but with different starter cultures, forms the first stage of cheese making. Another extensive application of microorganisms to food processing is the use of yeasts to transfer carbohydrates into alcohol and carbon dioxide, a key step in the production of beer, cider, wine, spirits and vinegar.

Equally important is the part yeast plays in the fermentation of sugars formed from wheat starch in bread making. The carbon dioxide released in this reaction expands the dough and, in traditional bread making processes, the gas is retained within the wheat protein structure giving a loaf of good texture and volume.

Novel food sources   The last twenty years have seen extensive attempts to create new raw food materials, and from them new foods, by growing microorganisims (yeasts and other fungi or bacteria) on cheap sources of organic carbon such as methane, other oil-derived hydrocarbons, starch residues and degraded cellulose. These new food sources are extensively tested and analysed for their nutritional content. Several foods incorporating a fungal protein (mycoprotein) are now commercially available.

GENERAL NUTRITIONAL ASPECTS

When considering the effects of processing on the nutritional value of food, it is important to bear in mind that food, particularly unprocessed food, is subject to spoilage and that this spoilage is often accompanied by a deterioration in the nutritional quality of the food. One of the advantages of processing is that it can arrest spoilage and so give a food of a more predictable nutritional content. By maintaining seasonal and geographical availability, processing greatly increases the chance of achieving a nutritionally adequate diet at all times of the year and in all areas of the world.

The degree of concern given to the loss of specific nutrients in various processes must also be considered within the context of the diet as a whole. In general, studies in this area have tended to focus on nutrients of importance in particular foods. Fresh meat, for example, is usually a significant contributor to the intake of riboflavin, thiamin and nicotinic acid (niacin) in the UK diet. Any loss of these vitamins which occurs as a result of processing may be important for those individuals relying on processed meat and meat products as the major source of these nutrients.

In contrast, the loss of vitamin C (ascorbic acid) in processed meat and its products would not normally be considered significant, as these products in their fresh forms are not usually a primary source of this vitamin. If, however, appreciable losses of ascorbic acid were to result from the processing of citrus fruits and juices or potatoes (important sources of vitamin C in the UK diet) then this would be a cause for concern.

When discussing processing losses, comparison is often made between raw foods, fresh from farm, garden or slaughterhouse, and those processed and then stored for long periods of time. Such comparisons are misleading. For example, if the effect of blanching on the level of a nutrient in a food is to be examined, the correct comparison might be between blanched, unstored product and the fresh, unstored product. Similarly, estimates of freezing losses should be made by comparing blanched, frozen, unstored samples and blanched, unfrozen and unstored samples. Often the losses sustained as a result of processing are in place of, rather than in addition to, those that occur in the home. This is why comparison of the food 'on the plate', as they would be eaten is important, for example fresh peas may require boiling for up to 10 minutes until they are tender, whilst frozen peas may only require $3^1/_2$ minutes boiling and canned peas only a brief reheating. By and large, the level of nutrients in most foods 'on the plate' when compared with their fresh equivalent are remarkably similar given normal storage conditions and processing techniques.

Losses of nutrients can be reported in a variety of ways. The most usual method of expressing loss is as a percentage of the original content of the nutrient in the food. Ideally, samples for analysis should be taken from the same cultivar (that is, the same variety, crop, soil growing conditions and geographical area), of similar size and harvested at the same time and degree of maturity. To some extent, such selectivity can counter the wide natural variation which occurs in the nutrient content of foods.

The data in Tables 1, 2, 3, and 4 have attempted to analyse the composition of certain samples of fresh and processed peas and potatoes as they would be eaten 'on the plate', but on a dry weight basis taking into account the appropriate domestic cooking times. As with most studies of this type, the data has certain limitations; but they do give an indication of general trends and are useful in this context.

Taking the example of garden peas, it is evident that conventional of

Table 1 Effect of storage and cooking on the proximate composition of garden peas (on a dry weight basis)

Sample	Protein %	Vitamin C mg/100g (%)[b]		K	Fe	Zn
					mg/100g	
Raw	25	130	(100)	1201	9.6	4.3
Cooked (12min) :						
with minimum water	26	116	(89)	930	9.3	4.2
with equal water	22	84	(65)	741	7.4	3.7
Stored[a] in pod 1 day then cooked (12 min) with minimum water	24	90	(69)	959	6.9	3.7
4 days then overcooked (18 min) with minimum water	15	57	(44)	915	6.8	3.6

[a] Stored at ambient temperature
[b] Percentage retention compared with raw sample
[c] Cooked in an equal volume of water
[d] Cooked in a minimum volume of water unless otherwise stated
[e] Figures obtained were the average of several analyses
(Source: Campden Food Preservation Research Association, 1987)

cooking has an appreciable affect on the content of vitamin C (which is subject to both leaching into the cooking water and destruction by heat) and some minerals but has little effect on the protein content unless the cooking is prolonged (Table 1). A modest storage period (4 days) followed by some overcooking led to an ultimate vitamin C content half that of the raw product. While frozen peas showed a comparable vitamin C content (Table 2), further losses were avoided on frozen storage. Canning resulted in a slight further reduction (Table 3) but, again, little further loss was seen on storage.

In contrast, the cooking of potatoes (Table 4) led to a substantial loss

Table 2   Effect of freezing and frozen storage on the proximate composition of garden peas (on a dry weight basis)

Sample	Protein (%)	Vitamin C mg/100g (%)[b]		K	Fe	Zn	Ca
					mg/100g		
Frozen and then cooked[d] (4 min)	26[c]	65	(50)	452	7.4	3.2	258
Cooked[d] after frozen storage time of:							
3 months	26[c]	61	(47)	672	7.1	3.5	288
6 months	25	58	(45)	755	6.7	3.6	272
9 months	24[c]	63	(48)	328	5.8	3.2	259

(See Table 1 for Footnotes)
(Source: Campden Food Preservation Research Association, 1987)

Table 3   Effects of canning and canned storage on the proximate composition of garden peas (on a dry weight basis)

Sample	Protein (%)	Vitamin C mg/100g (%)[b]		K	Fe	ZN	Ca
					mg/100g		
Canned and then cooked (5 min)	24	50	(38)	426	6.9	3.0	198
Cooked[d] after canned storage time of:							
3 months	25	40	(31)	673	7.0	3.0	201
6 months	24	37	(28)	698	6.5	2.8	186
9 months	24	38	(29)	359	6.7	2.9	182

(See Table 1 for footnotes)
(Source: Campden Food Preservation Research Association, 1987)

vitamin C and conventional storage of the raw vegetable led to considerable further losses. Frozen chipped potatoes compared well in this regard with their fresh equivalent and with boiled.

Table 4   Effect of storage[2] and cooking on the proximate constituents of old potatoes (on a dry weight basis)

Sample	Protein (%)	Vitamin C[e] (mg/100g)	K (mg/100g)	Ca (mg/100g)	Zn (mg/100g)
Zero time					
Raw	10.1	<57	1590	34.7	1.4
Fried (chipped) (cooked 190°C/10mins)	7.7	<16	964	23.1	1.1
3 Months Storage					
Raw	11.4	<15	1787	27.7	0.7
Boiled (equal water)	9.8	< 7	948	42.5	1.0
Fried (chipped)	7.3	<20	1248	21.9	1.1
6 Months Storage					
Raw	10.4	<13	1268	15.7	1.3
Boiled	9.1	<22	1102	31.8	1.1
Fried (chipped)	8.2	< 6	1500	19.5	0.4
Fried (frozen chipped) (cooked 190°C/3mins)	6.7	<20	1132	40.4	0.6
9 Months Storage					
Raw	12.0		2857	17.0	1.8
Boiled	11.6		2451	29.0	1.5
Fried (chipped)	8.3		1801	16.9	0.9
Fried (frozen chipped) (3 months)	7.3	<18	1292	28.6	1.1
Fried (frozen chipped) (6 months)	8.4	<14	1139	38.5	1.2

(See Table 1 for footnotes)   (Source: Camden Food Preservation Research Association, 1987)

EFFECTS ON FOODS OF PHYSICAL METHODS OF PROCESSING

This section discusses in more detail the main physical agents used in food processing together with some information on their effects.

Effect of heat on food

The early discovery that heat produces changes in raw foodstuffs that makes them more acceptable to eat, and also affords some degree of preservation, was of prime importance to the health and social development of primitive man. Today's modern food industry uses equipment that may appear to be very different from traditional cooking methods, but its basic purpose remains the same. Heat is still used as a method of preservation, sometimes with minimal changes in eating quality (for example, the pasteurisation of milk). Heating is also an integral part of the evaporation, distillation and drying processes. Although the overall consequences of heating foods are very complex, some of the main changes in foods and their components are indicated below.

Action on microorganisms

The destruction of microorganisms is a highly important and much studied aspect of the application of heat to foodstuffs. Microorganisms can spoil the flavour and appearance of a food and some can cause food poisoning. Yeasts and other fungi are readily killed by moderate heating, as are many species of bacteria. Some bacterial species, however, can exist as spores which resist the destructive action of heat. In appropriate conditions, the spore may later become active and generate rapidly multiplying bacteria.

Normal cooking procedures owe much of their preservative effect to their action in reducing the number of live microorganisms present. However, only intensive heating practices (such as those used in processing canned meat, fish and vegetable products) approaches the total destruction of all organisms.

Clostridium botulinum is an organism that has received much attention both because of the lethal nature of the toxin it produces and because its spores are extremely resistant to destruction by heat. If the degree of heating is sufficient to destroy all *Clostridium botulinum* spores, no other food poisoning organisms can survive.

Clostridium botulinum fails to grow in acid conditions (pH below 4.5), such as those that occur in some canned fruits, and its growth is impeded by the presence of curing salts (nitrates and nitrites) in, for example, ham and bacon. As a result, these products generally require only a modest heat treatment. As *Clostridium botulinum* grows only in the virtual absence of oxygen, the appropriate combination of conditions for clostridial growth occurs in canned products or in products packaged in impermeable containers. Fully effective and controlled heat processing methods are therefore essential for such products. The safety record of canned foods demonstrates that the requisite conditions are almost always achieved. Most of the very rare outbreaks of botulism from canned goods have been due to secondary contamination after damage to the can.

Foods subject to microbial spoilage should never be held for any length of time between the temperatures of 10–63°C, generally regarded as the optimum range for microbial growth. Such temperature conditions should not occur in the planned and controlled operations of the food industry, but constant vigilance is required to ensure that during the manufacture, distribution and retail sale of foods, the correct procedures are always followed. When outbreaks of food poisoning do occur, the cause is usually attributable to poor hygiene within the home or in catering establishments. However, the scale of production in the food processing industry, and hence the potential for infection, emphasises the need for strict adherence to impeccable practices of hygiene and manufacture.

Effects on the plant cell wall

The texture of many plant foods is largely dependent on the structure and arrangement of their cell walls. Breakdown and partial solubilising of the complex molecules (for example, pectin) that make up the cell walls occurs when the foods are heated in water. If the changes are not allowed to proceed too far, the softening that results from this breakdown process

Table 5   Stability of nutrients

Nutrient	Effect of pH			Air or Oxygen	Light	Heat
	Neutral	Acid	Alkaline			
Vitamins						
Vitamin A	S	U	S	U	U	U
Ascorbic acid (C)	U	S	U	U	U	U
Biotin	S	S	S	S	S	U
Carotene (pro-A)	S	U	S	U	U	U
Cobalamin (B_{12})	S	S	S	U	U	S
Vitamin D	S		U	U	U	U
Folic acid	U	U	S	U	U	U
Vitamin K	S	U	U	S	U	S
Niacin	S	S	S	S	S	S
Pantothenic acid	S	U	U	S	S	U
Pyridoxine (B_6)	S	S	S	S	U	U
Riboflavin (B_2)	S	S	U	S	U	U
Thiamin (B_1)	U	S	U	U	S	U
Tocopherol (E)	S	S	S	U	U	U
Essential amino acids						
Isoleucine	S	S	S	S	S	S
Leucine	S	S	S	S	S	S
Lysine	S	S	S	S	S	U
Methionine	S	S	S	S	S	S
Phenylalanine	S	S	S	S	S	S
Threonine	S	U	U	S	S	U
Tryptophan	S	U	S	S	U	S
Valine	S	S	S	S	S	S
Essential fatty acids	S	S	U	U	U	S
Mineral salts	S	S	S	S	S	S

S   Stable (no important destruction)

U   Unstable (significant destruction)

(Source: Harris and Karmas, 1975)

can create agreeable textures and improved palatability (for example, cooked green vegetables).

Effects on nutrients

Proteins   The heating of proteins results in a disorganisation of their structure (denaturation). This does not usually reduce the biological value of the proteins and in many cases acts positively by increasing protein digestibility.

During heating some amino acids (particularly lysine) can react with reducing sugars (glucose and fructose) in the 'Maillard" or non-enzymic browning reactions. These reactions are responsible for many of the desirable changes in colour and flavour that occur during cooking, for example the crust on baked bread. With mild heating the loss of available lysine is small but as the heating becomes more severe and browning more pronounced losses of lysine may be marked and can be accompanied by small reductions in the availability of other amino acids. These losses, however, are unlikely to be of great nutritional significance for those people eating a varied and adequate diet.

Carbohydrates   The solubilisation of starch granules in the presence of water and heat improves the digestibility of many staple foods such as potatoes, bread, rice and cereal products. The dextrinisation of starch and caramelisation of sugars in dry heating conditions are responsible for many of the characteristic colours and flavours we associate with cooked foods.

Fats   Fats and oils, particularly those rich in unsaturated fatty acids, are prone to oxidative change during heating in air. The use of natural or synthetic antioxidants protects against the undesirable changes that can result so that losses in nutritional content are unlikely to be significant.

Vitamins   Many studies on the effect of heating on nutrients have focussed on vitamin retention. Some vitamins, particulary vitamin C (ascorbic acid) and vitamin B_1 (thiamin), readily indergo chemical reactions which can reduce the amount of vitamin present in the food. Due to their sensitivity, vitamin losses after heat treatment are used as an indicator; if such losses are within acceptable limits, it is considered that the other nutrients present will be largely unaffected.

Vitamin C is easily oxidised in the presence of heat and atmospheric oxygen to dehydroascorbic acid (DHA) without loss of vitamin activity. This intermediate can in turn be irreversibly converted to diketogulonic acid, a compound having no biological activity.

As a substantial fraction of the intake of vitamin C in most diets comes from fresh fruit and vegetables, fruit juices and home-cooked vegetables (which retain much of their vitamin C), losses of vitamin C during industrial processing, while requiring to be minimised, are unlikely to affect greatly the total intake of this nutrient for the majority of the population who are eating a varied diet. Commercially canned citrus fruits and juices (pH < 4.5) do not usually require severe heat treatment and consequently retention of vitamin C in these products is high.

At the temperatures generally used in can sterilisation, vitamin C can be rapidly destroyed. The destruction is aggravated when residual oxygen is present in the headspace of the can. The type of container that is used also affects the level of vitamin C in the final product. Though seldom used nowadays, in unlacquered cans, a portion of the oxygen trapped in the can is consumed in reactions between the tin-plate and any acid that may be present in the food. In lacquered cans, however, the reaction with the container is inhibited and most of the residual oxygen is available to react with the vitamin C in the product. On storage of canned foods, some leaching of water-soluble nutrients into the liquor can occur. This is only a loss to the consumer if the liquor is discarded. Table 6 shows typical values for the retention of some vitamins in vegetables after blanching and then after heat processing the cans.

Large losses of vitamins can occur in catering operations where there is overcooking or long holding-times involved in meal preparation. When vegetables are kept hot for several hours, almost total loss of vitamin C occurs, together with losses of other vitamins. In parallel with these losses, the eating quality of the food deteriorates extensively. The design of catering systems to preserve both nutrient content and eating quality, by decentralisation or by use of cook/freeze or cook/chill techniques, makes possible improved nutrient retention (British Nutrition Foundation, 1985).

Table 6 Retention of ascorbic acid, thiamin, riboflavin, niacin and carotene in vegetable canning

Product vitamin	After blanching				After blanching and heat processing of can			
	Number of observations	Maximum (%)	Minimum (%)	Mean (%)	Number of observations	Maximum (%)	Minimum (%)	Mean (%)
Green beans								
Ascorbic acid	38	90	50	74	41	75	40	55
Thiamin	34	100	82	91	41	90	55	71
Riboflavin	29	100	70	95	30	100	85	96
Niacin	29	100	60	93	30	100	80	92
Carotene	—	—	—	—	9	96	81	87
Peas								
Ascorbic acid	60	90	60	76	43	90	45	72
Carotene	—	—	—	—	12	100	88	97
Thiamin	60	100	73	88	54	70	40	54
Riboflavin	37	87	67	75	43	100	70	82
Niacin	39	96	59	73	32	80	50	65
Spinach								
Ascorbic acid	21	78	39	61	21	62	34	52
Carotene	—	—	—	—	5	—	—	100
Thiamin	4	—	—	77	5	—	—	100
Riboflavin	4	—	—	81	5	—	—	76
Niacin	4	—	—	89	4	—	—	78

(Source: Lamb et el., 1982)

In controlled industrial processing, as in normal domestic cooking, some loss of vitamins is inevitable and unavoidable. In some cases, uncontrolled and excessive domestic cooking can cause vitamin losses greater than those found in industrial processes. The technology available to industry allows the restoration of nutrients lost during processing and this is widely practised, particularly by those manufacturing flour, margarines, cereal products and fruit juices.

Inorganic nutrients (including trace elements) Losses of minerals will occur by leaching into the cooking water. It is unlikely that such effects will be nutritionally important and inorganic salts are considered stable to heat processing.

Effects on enzymes

One group of proteins, the 'enzymes', initiate and accelerate many of the chemical reactions in living organisms. When untreated foods are transported or stored, the enzymes often bring about undesirable textural and flavour changes in the foods. The application of heat (blanching) inactivates enzymes that can cause deterioration during storage.

Blanching Blanching is an essential preliminary not only to canning but also to the freezing or drying of many foodstuffs. It involves a partial pre-cooking by immersion in hot water or treatment with steam. As well as inactivating enzymes that may cause deterioration during storage, blanching expels gas from the fibres of foods thereby rendering them more suitable for canning, reduces the number of microorganisims present and can also act as a method of cleansing.

As the process usually involves large amounts of water and free access to atmospheric oxygen, losses of nutrients may be expected. These may occur via oxidation (for example, vitamin C) and by leaching into the surrounding medium (for example, water-soluble vitamins and mineral salts, sugars and possibly some proteins). Leaching losses only become significant if the liquor is subsequently discarded.

A number of factors will affect the magnitude of loss of nutrients. These include the surface-to-mass ratio of the product (foods with a large surface area like broccoli and spinach are liable to encounter larger losses through leaching than, for example, brussels sprouts), the product-to-water ratio and the time and temperature of treatment. Other factors include the maturity and size of the food, younger, smaller fruits and vegetables losing more of certain nutrients than larger, more mature samples (Harris and von Loesecke, 1960).

For the maximum retention of nutrients during blanching, the shortest blanch, consistent with the attainment of a high quality product, at temperatures high enough to inactivate enzymes, but with minimum contact with air, is indicated. Extended holding periods between blanching and further processing (for example, filling exhausting or canning) can increase losses of vitamins (especially vitamin C). Further processing should therefore be undertaken with the minimum of delay.

Pasteurisation The aim of the process is to destroy undesirable pathogens in the product. Many of the less heat resistant spoilage organisms are also destroyed and this prolongs the storage life of the product. Milk is commonly pasteurised as in its raw state it is a highly perishable product.

Pasteurisation can be accomplished by one of two methods. The older 'Holder' process involves a temperature of 61–66°C for a period of 30 minutes. The newer high temperature short-time (HTST) treatment applies a temperature of 71–73°C for only 15 seconds. The latter is generally preferred as there is less damage to nutrients and less effect on flavour (see Table7).

Sterilisation of milk by the modern continuous flow ultra heat treatment process (130–150°C for1–4 seconds) results in effective bacterial destruction whilst minimising the chemical changes that produce nutrient losses (see Table 7). This process has been applied with most success to liquid foods, such as milk, which can be heated and cooled very quickly. After heating and cooling, the liquids are filled into sterilised containers under conditions that minimise contamination and so allow a storage life of several months.

Effect of storage

Although the manufacturer may take every precaution to guard against

Table 7 Effect of heat processing on vitamins in milk

Product/ process	A^b	D	B_1	B_2	Niacin	B_6	B_{12}^a	C	Folic $acid^c$	Pantothenic acid	Biotin
								Percentage retention of vitamins			
Whole milk											
Pasteurised (HTST)	100	100	90	100	100	100	90	$90\text{--}75^d$	90	100	100
Sterilised (in bottle)	100	100	65	100	100	50	10	10	50	100	100
UHT	100	100	90	100	100	90	90	75	90	100	100
Evaporated	100	100	60	100	95	60	20	40	75	100	90

[a] Vitamin B_{12} is stable to heat. Losses are caused by products of vitamin C destruction.
[b] Retinol equivalents.
[c] Total folic acid – free and bound.
[d] Samples stored in light with free access to oxygen will have levels at the lower end of the range.

(Source: Rolls, 1982)

nutrient loss during processing, his efforts can often be negated by inappropriate storage conditions which are beyond his control. It is important to be able to make some estimation of effects on nutrients during different storage conditions to ascertain the shelf life of the product for planning, distribution and for labelling purposes.

A number of factors will influence the effect of storage on nutrients. The temperature of storage, the atmosphere within and without the food package, the amount of exposure to light, and the length of time in storage (sensitive nutrients showing a progressive decrease over time) are all important.

The retention of protein, carbohydrate, minerals and fat is largely unchanged by storage. In acid products sucrose may undergo hydrolysis but this has only a minor effect on the nutritional value.

A slow loss of the heat-labile vitamins can occur during high temperature storage. This can be due to a leaching into the surrounding medium which may be a loss if the liquor is subsequently discarded or as a consequence of slow anaerobic breakdown. The effect varies with the nature of the product and is more pronounced in non-acid than acid products. A low temperature storage would seem to be indicated for products providing valuable sources of the more sensitive vitamins, for example canned fruit juices, fruits and vegetables, and meat products. If extended storage periods are envisaged (greater than 2 years), the temperature becomes even more crucial and the exclusion of oxygen and/or the use of antioxidants is indicated.

The use of cooling for food preservation

The primary purposes of lowering the temperature of a food are, firstly, to reduce the rates of chemical and physical changes, and, secondly, to arrest or at least slow down the growth of unwanted or harmful microorganisms. Refrigeration is now so familiar to consumers that the industrial use of cold conditions for similar purposes is not regarded by most consumers as 'processing'. The use of the 'cold chain' in the collection of raw materials, in distribution, storage and display for sale by retailers is equally widely used and accepted,

In the catering industry there has been a rapid growth in the use of cook/chill systems, in which precooked food is stored for limited periods at appropriate low temperatures prior to reheating and service. The safe operation of this system requires efficient control of temperatures, strict adherence to specified storage times and hence a high degree of training.

The effects of low temperature storage on foods suggests that their use, even for the storage and transport of raw foods, should properly be regarded as a form of processing. Food held at low temperatures is still capable of undergoing change, albeit at a reduced rate, so that the product cannot be exactly compared with its fresh equivalent. Fortunately, it is exceptional for the disturbance in reaction rates to affect quality materially, but instances can arise. Meat that is chilled quickly after the slaughter of the animal can undergo 'cold shortening', resulting in toughening of the meat. This effect is intensified if the meat is removed from the bone before chilling, but can be partially overcome by prior electrical stimulation of the carcase. The electrical treatment accelerates some of the normal post-mortem changes, making it possible to chill the meat only a short time after slaughter without it developing toughness. Early chilling clearly has hygienic advantages, but to secure these benefits, meat has to undergo some 'processing'.

Low temperatures can also interfere with the normal ripening of some tropical or sub-tropical fruits. The storage of bananas below about 11°C (the precise temperature depends on the time of storage and on the banana variety) distorts the development of the fruit so that the tissues break down when the temperature is raised and the fruit becomes inedible. To allow bananas to survive the long journey by sea from the West Indies, they are picked slightly unripe and cooled to just above the critical temperature of 11°C. On reaching their destination, the temperature is raised to allow the ripening process to be completed.

Thus, even when the effects of processing are not apparent in the foods as purchased, there is often a history of processing. The use of low temperatures is essential to preserve desirable qualities and to extend the useful life of many foods. Without such 'processing' these foods would have restricted areas of distribution and would be very seasonal in availability.

Effects of freezing on food

Until mechanised refrigeration became available at the end of the 19th century, foods could only be frozen in any quantity in areas of the world where external temperatures were below $0°C$ or where ice and snow were available to permit freezing mixtures of ice and salt to be made. Although frozen fish and meat were familiar, and useful, in arctic conditions, in the UK, frozen foods were restricted to a few luxuries served in wealthy households or expensive restaurants.

In the last eighty years, and especially since the Second World War, freezing has become a key process for the preservation of both raw and cooked foods. The temperatures normally used for frozen storage (-18 to $-30°C$) are such that no microbiological growth can occur. However, many species of microorganisms can survive freezing and frozen storage and are therefore able to grow and multiply in or on the food after it has been thawed. Most chemical changes in food are slowed down during frozen storage to the point where they virtually cease to occur. Some others (e.g. fat oxidation and some enzymically stimulated reactions) still occur, although more slowly. These latter reactions limit the storage life of some frozen foods such as fatty fish.

The need to blanch most vegetables prior to freezing, in order to inactivate some enzymes, has already been mentioned. For cooked foods, normal cooking destroys all the enzymes originally present, but fat oxidation can still occur when the cooked foods are stored in the frozen state. This can be avoided by the use of antioxidants and also by the scrupulous exclusion of iron and copper contamination, since these metals catalyse the reactions.

The sequence of changes that occurs within foods as they undergo freezing is highly complex. In raw foods, the water holding capacity of the cellular structures can be affected and, on thawing, the water may be released, as 'drip'. This is a familiar consequence of freezing, and is most noticeable in frozen poultry or meats. Rapid freezing and very low storage temperatures can minimise losses due to 'drip' in both raw and cooked foods whilst still preserving quality, so that the correctly thawed or reheated food closely matches the fresh or cooked food prior to freezing. These methods form the basis of the very effective 'cook/freeze' system of catering, which has considerably modified institutional catering systems and has provided greater flexibility in commercial catering. This system has been shown to improve the retention of vitamin C (provided that rapid reheating is employed) when compared with conventional systems involving significant warmholding periods (Hunt, 1984).

The key discovery, from which the modern frozen food industry has grown, was that quality was improved when freezing time was reduced ('quick freezing'). Factors affecting freezing time include the efficiency of heat transfer, the size and shape of the food or packages and the water content of the food. Modern techniques have the advantage of minimising internal water movement which results in reduced tissue damage. For foods that are small in volume (for example, peas), very rapid freezing is achieved by passing a current of cold air through the food, creating a 'fluidised bed'. As a result, quick frozen peas are, after thawing, self-evidently 'fresher' in appearance and in eating quality than peas in the pod that have passed through the normal distribution chain for sale by a retail greengrocer. For other foods, blast freezing, in which cold air is blown vigorously over the surfaces of the food or food package, gives fairly rapid and controlled freezing. Recently the potential advantages of using sprays of liquid nitrogen in a continuous freezer, to give very rapid freezing, have been explored. Frozen foods offer a high degree of convenience. The apparent high cost of frozen cooked foods and frozen complete meals, is largely or wholly cancelled out when the true labour and fuel costs of the domestic kitchen are taken into account. The use of frozen foods has greatly increased in recent times and this is likely to continue as domestic freezers become as common as refrigerators.

Effects on nutrients

The nutritive value of frozen foods can in most cases closely match the quality of the equivalent 'fresh' product (Tables 2 and 4). In some. the level of particular nutrients may even be higher. For example peas, designated for freezing, tend to be harvested and processed within the space of a few hours, whereas peas termed 'market fresh' may, in fact, have been stored at ambient temperature for several days, so considerably diminishing the levels of some nutrients (for example, vitamin C).

When comparing the nutritive value of frozen and fresh foods, the most relevant comparison is between two samples of food fully prepared for eating. Comparing the samples uncooked ignores the likelihood that the fresh samples often require a longer cooking time to achieve acceptable palatability.

Effect of storage

Some loss of vitamins can occur during frozen storage, the magnitude of loss depending on the product, the prefreezing treatment (especially blanching), the type of packaging and the storage conditions (Fennema, 1982). The temperature of storage must be a balance between the optimal for preventing damage and the practical attainable temperature and is usually −18°C. At this temperature deterioration proceeds only very slowly.

Some vitamins are particularly susceptible to relatively minor changes in storage temperature. For example, at −18°C there is a relatively slow loss of Vitamin C. An increase to −10°C can result in a 2– to 5–fold increase in the rate of loss of this vitamin (Fennema, 1975). Even at temperatures as low as −30°C some loss occurs. The type of packaging used during storage is very important and losses of vitamin C are minimised if a material with low oxygen permeability is used.

Effect of thawing

The initial rate of freezing will influence subsequent losses of nutrients on thawing. During thawing, losses of nutrients can occur but are very variable as the process usually occurs in the home under uncontrolled conditions. Losses of water-soluble vitamins and minerals occur as a result of the migration of water and other components during freezing and thawing which results in an exudate or drip.

The use of evaporation and the drying of food

The evaporation of liquid from foods (that is, reduction in water content) is used as a stage in the preparation of many food products. The reduction in bulk achieved by the evaporation of water facilitates easy storage and transport of foodstuffs. In some foods, the increased concentration of soluble stubstances (for example, sugars), resulting from evaporation, is sufficient to reduce substantially the availability of water to microorganisms. The process has in consequence some preservation action. Concentrated sugar solutions, for example, will keep almost idefinitely even at ambient temperatures, so that they can be transported in tankers and stored in a form ready for immediate use in food manufacture.

Fruit juices are commonly evaporated to allow transport of large quantities over long distances, from the fruit growing areas to user countries. The concentrated juice can then be diluted to single strength for packaging and retail sale. It may also be converted into nectars and 'drinks' containing a proportion of fruit juice. The heat used to evaporate fruit juices can cause undesirable flavour changes and the energy costs of simple evaporation are high. Vacuum evaporation, which employs lower temperatures, and modern evaporator designs that increase the water evaporated per unit of applied heat, have been successful in retaining reasonable juice quality while substantially reducing energy usage.

Some loss of volatile flavour components occurs during evaporation. However, where the improvement in quality justifies the additional cost, a proportion of these substances can be recovered and added to the juice at an appropriate stage. Differences in juice quality reflect the quality of the fruit employed and the skill and care with which all heat treatments and storage operations are carried out. One of the main nutrients of fruit juice (apart from sugars) is vitamin C. The destruction of vitamin C by heat during modern evaporation processes has been reduced to an acceptable level and losses of the vitamin on storage are minimized by the exclusion of oxygen during packing.

Evaporation is used in the preparation of condensed and evaporated milk and as the first stage in the preparation of dried milk. As with fruit juice, processes are designed to minimise vitamin destruction and to avoid heat damage to the other components of the milk. Even when great care is taken, traces of 'burnt' flavour are readily detected in evaporated milk (115°C for 15 minutes), especially when compared with the bland flavour of unheated milk. Vitamin losses in milk during evaporation tend to be greater than those that arise in modern methods of pasteurisation (see

Table 7). Even with careful selection of the conditions, the preservative action of evaporation is limited.

The objectives of drying are similar to evaporation, but in contrast drying is a very effective means of preservation. If sufficiently complete, drying can totally inhibit microbial growth, which is suspended owing to the lack of available water. Some microorganisms are reduced in numbers by the lethal action of particular stages of the drying process and some are destroyed during dry storage, especially in the early stages. Yeasts and moulds and most bacteria have their activity completely suspended by dry conditions, but remain viable and can recommence growth when water is subsequently added.

Drying sharply reduces the rate of many chemical reactions that occur in foods, including those that are enzyme assisted. Fat oxidation may be enhanced by the conditions created by intensive drying. Consequently, care is required to achieve an optimal moisture content for the best overall performance of such foods during prolonged storage in sealed containers.

The drying of solid foodstuffs, especially those based on intact plant or animal tissues (meat, fish, vegetables and fruit) is a very complex process. The biological structure may collapse irreversibly, as water is removed. Dissolved substances that are held within cells may migrate during drying, so causing further changes. These changes are not always reversed when water is added back to the dried food. Research continues into ways of improving flavour and texture in reconstituted dried products.

Fish, meat and fruit have long been dried to facilitate long term storage, but almost invariably these products have been so modified by drying that they cannot adequately be used to replace the fresh foodstuffs, although dried fish and meat may serve valuable purposes in developing countries by giving flavour to bland cereal products and soups. Dried fruits, such as currants, raisins, figs, dates and apricots, although different in texture from the fruits from which they have been prepared, are acceptable for their own eating qualities and have many culinary uses. The higher sugar content of these foods reduces the structural damage that may occur as a consequence of drying, and at the same time allows an effective means of preservation without the need to proceed to total dryness.

Among the important groups of raw foodstuffs which dry naturally are the cereal seeds, seed of legumes such as peas and the many varieties of beans, nuts, spices, and coffee beans. The use of artificial drying to replace or enhance natural drying need not produce changes which are different from those resulting from the natural process, provided that the temperatures and the rates of drying are tightly controlled. The smaller the particles of food, the more readily can they be dried and, in general, the less structural and nutrient damage will result. The various dried seeds can then be stored for long periods, without appreciable deterioration. Partly for this reason, they constitute the major fraction of the world's food reserves.

When peas dry naturally on the plant, the end product (13% moisture) differs sharply from peas at the stage of optimum eating quality (nearly 80% moisture). Naturally dried peas have their own place as a foodstuff, but are regarded as a different product from fresh and frozen peas and from canned 'garden peas'. Many attempts have been made to reduce the changes caused when peas, picked at optimum conditions, are artifically dried. Perhaps the most successful technique involved piercing each pea prior to drying, which allows the water in the interior of the peas to pass to the drying air much more readily, so that the pea tissue is less exposed to heat. When peas dried in this manner are reconstituted with water and cooked, their final state approaches but does not quite match the quality of cooked fresh or frozen peas. Despite allowing long term stable storage at room temperature, dried peas have had only limited commercial success.

For liquids, such as milk and extracted coffee, spray drying (that is, the rapid air drying of small droplets) has proved a very useful process. However, one disadvantage of the spray-dried product has been the difficulty in rewetting the fine dry particles. This has been partly overcome by aggregating groups of particles by means of an additional process. Such products are called 'instantised' to reflect their ready dispersion in water, but, even so, the reconstituted spray-dried food cannot always match the quality or range of use of the untreated product.

Freeze drying

In freeze drying the material is first frozen and then subjected to a mild heating process in a vacuum cabinet. The ice crystals formed during freezing sublime when heated under reduced pressure. The immobilisation of the food structure by freezing reduces the extent of damage resulting from the removal of water during the drying stage. The removal of the water leaves a network of holes (pores) which, on reconstitution, permit the rapid entry of water. In these circumstances, the moisture content is restored to almost its original level. Additionally, some products may be packaged in a nitrogen atmosphere to reduce the oxidation of fat. The new process has been applied experimentally to many vegetables, with considerable technical success, although the results with meat and fish have been less satisfactory. Commercially freeze-dried products have had to compete with quick frozen foods, which require fewer stages of manufacture, are generally superior in quality and are cheaper. Consequently, most freeze-dried solid foods have been withdrawn from the market. The application of freeze drying to liquid foods, such as coffee extract, has proved much more successful, as the process gives a high degree of flavour retention.

Effects of drying on nutrients

Losses of nutrients occur during the stages that precede the actual drying. Sample temperature, moisture content, rate of drying and exposure time are all important factors in determining the extent of nutrient loss in the process itself. As the process involves a temperature and concentration gradient, it is to be expected that nutrient loss will not be uniformly distributed throughout the product. Average nutrient retention is the important criterion in practice.

As most drying operations are performed in the presence of oxygen, some vitamin destruction, especially vitamin C, is to be expected. The use of antioxidants has considerably reduced losses which arise in this way. Potatoes constitute an important source of vitamin C and, consequently, most manufacturers of 'instant' mashed potato make good the loss of vitamin C by supplementing the vitamin to the final product. This makes it a more reliable source of vitamin C than home cooked potatoes which have their vitamin C content reduced during storage of the raw potatoes and the susequent cooking.

Carotenes, including those with provitamin A activity, are well retained during dehydration when the vegetable has been previously blanched, as this significantly reduces losses due to enzymic action. Today's modern methods of drying achieve almost total retention for this group of substances. Freeze drying, in particular, is adjudged the best method for vitamin retention.

Effect of storage

Non-enzymic browning and oxidation are, in general, the predominant mechanisms for loss of nutritional value in stored, dehydrated foods. These undesirable reactions can be avoided to some extent by the use of appropriate packaging materials which are either chemically inert or have low permeability to moisture and gases. Packaging under vacuum or inert gas and the addition of an in-packaging desiccant or oxygen scavenger may be alternative methods of retarding deterioration.

The storage temperature is an important factor governing the retention of vitamins in dehydrated foods. Long-term storage should ideally be at a temperature of $0°C$ or less. Dehydrated eggs benefit from frozen storage if levels of vitamin A are to be maintained for longer than 1 month.

The use of radiation on food

Many parts of the electromagnetic spectrum play some part in food processing. In ordinary heating operations, infra red radiation, from hot surfaces or flames, makes some energy contribution, supplementing conduction, convection and the latent heat derived from steam condensation. Current interest centres on the use of microwaves for cooking and the use of ionising radiation for preservation.

Irradiation

The term 'irradiation', as it relates to food, has come to mean the treatment of foods, for a variety of purposes, with high energy electromagnetic radiation and/or electrons, provided by radioisotopes, high voltage particle generators or short wavelength X-ray machines. Such radiations are conveniently referred to collectively as 'ionizing radiation', a term which illustrates one of their most important properties, the production of charged particles (ions) in the substances exposed to them. The ions produced undergo various reactions leading to chemical changes in the material irradiated. The changes which occur at the doses recommended are not considered a hazard to human health (DHSS, 1986).

The words 'irradiated food' often brings to the mind of the consumer, associations with the adverse effects of the radiation connected with power generation from atomic energy or indeed from nuclear explosions. This false analogy arises due to a lack of detailed knowledge of the types and properties of the various radiations and of the effects they have on different organisms and substances.

Some applications of irradiation to foods require only low doses while others require heavier doses. The applications most intensively studied are, in order of increasing dose requirement, inhibition of sprouting (for example, potatoes, onions), insect disinfestation (for example, cereals, cocoa beans, pulses, spices), delay of ripening (for example, bananas), general reduction in microbiological load especially on the food surface (for example, fruit, vegetables, meat, fish), reduction in non-spore forming pathogenic bacteria, (for example, fish, meat and their products), sterilisation (for example, fish meat and their products) and the elimination of viruses.

In the next few years food irradiation will be a subject of increased popular interest. Both nationally and internationally it is likely that a number of uses of irradiation will be proposed and some irradiated foods will appear in the market place. This position has been reached only after extensive research in many countries, extending over a period of some 50 years.

Concern over the safety of irradiated foods is two-fold. The prime aspect of public concern is whether the food, after irradiation, has itself become radioactive, so that it is itself a source of radiation. The facts are quite clear. If the radioactive source is cobalt–60 or caesium–137, then the energy of the radiation is not sufficient to cause any significant induced radioactivity. Even if the energy of the radiation were some ten-fold higher, the effect would still be entirely negligible and indeed undetectable. If machine sources of radiation are used, higher energies are possible, and it is necessary to set an upper limit to the permitted energy of irradiation. No residual radioactivity could then occur in the food. Although much will still be written on this aspect of food irradiation, the facts have been established by experiment beyond scientific doubt.

The second aspect is more complex to study. High energy radiation causes chemical changes in food by direct action on food molecules and principally by indirect action on the water in moist foods. Typically free radicals are produced which are highly reactive and short-lived. As a result a variety of chemical reactions are induced in foods, producing small quantities of a number of chemical substances not previously present. From the safety point of view, this action can be regarded as equivalent to adding these chemicals to the food. The amounts formed are proportional to the magnitude of dose of radiation absorbed by the food, a quantity that can be measured. The nature of the chemical substances formed depends on the composition of the irradiated food. Exhaustive toxicological tests in many laboratories and countries, for a wide range of foodstuffs, have confirmed the complete safety for consumption of foods that have received dose levels up to at least 1 Mrad (10 kGy). Indeed the Joint FAO/IAEA/WHO Expert Committee on the 'Wholesomeness of Irradiated Food' concluded in 1981 that 'the irradiation of any food commodity up to an overall average dose of 10 kGy (that is, 1 Mrad) presents no toxicological hazard; hence, toxicological testing of foods so treated is no longer required'. In 1986 the DHSS report on the *Safety and Wholesomeness of Irradiated Foods* came to a similar conclusion. This is, of course, a scientific judgement, whereas the actual control of irradiated foods is a matter requiring regulation in each country. Effective inhibition of sprouting and insect disinfestation can be achieved at average doses of less than one tenth of the 1 Mrad figure. Doses up to 1 Mrad are sufficient for a substantial reduction in the numbers of spoilage and pathogenic bacteria and fungi. Spores of pathogenic bacteria are likely to survive the treatment so that adequate microbial evaluation of the process and the subsequent storage conditions will still be required.

Effects on nutrients

Nutrient losses due to irradiation up to 1 Mrad level are mostly small, although some attention has been directed to losses of vitamin C in orange juice and in stored, irradiated potatoes. The DHSS report (1986) concluded that 'irradiation of food at the appropriate dose, up to an overall average dose of 10 kGy, will not have any special adverse effects on its nutritional content'. The report considered that, should the process be permitted in the UK, its usage and any nutritional consequences (in the light of consumption patterns) should be monitored.

The application of food irradiation up to an average dose of 1 Mrad (10 kGy) used, either alone or in combination with other modes of preservation, offers new options to the food industry that may well enhance the quality and shelf life of a number of foods, with accompanying benefit to the consumer. Complete sterilisation, including the destruction of bacterial spores, requires average dose levels up to 5 Mrad (50 kGy). This level poses greater problems of chemical change, toxicological testing, off-flavour production and nutrient destruction. It has been used extensively where diets require complete sterilisation (for example, patients with reduced immunocompetence) without adverse effect, but is unlikely to be developed commercially.

Microwave heating

In conventional cooking, heat applied to the outside of a food by conduction, convection or radiation is conducted to the interior of the food. In contrast, food cooked by microwaves involves the use of heat generated from within the food through the absorption of the microwave radiation by molecules, in particular by water molecules. The ability to heat through the thickness of a food, combined with short heating times (often of the order of one minute), offers interesting possibilities for use in food processing, catering and domestic cooking.

Rapid heating of chilled, thawed or frozen foods by microwaves can reduce microbiological risks when compared with incorrect conventional heating. However, the very high capital cost per unit of energy transferred suggests that only specialised uses will be found for microwave heating in food manufacture. The appearance of food cooked by microwaves (pale, due to lack of browning) and the texture (more moist and dense especially in baked goods) is not always readily accepted by many consumers. Combination with convection heating or special end cookers goes some way to remedy this problem. The microwave radiation is unable to penetrate through metals, so careful designs of ovens and other heaters is necessary to allow heating of the food as well as to provide complete protection for the operator. The value and limitations of microwave heating are currently being tested by extensive use in the home and by caterers.

Effects on nutrients

Like other heating processes, nutrient losses are to be expected, but there are several factors which suggest that microwave cooking or the use of microwaves in food processing might minimise the loss of some nutrients. When the process was originally developed, it was considered likely that the shorter heating and holding times would reduce the loss of heat-labile nutrients. Similarly, since less cooking water is required, the loss through leaching of water-soluble nutrients should be reduced. It was therefore anticipated that there would be some considerable benefit associated with the use of microwave heating.

These expectations have proved difficult to confirm. Assessment of the reported work on nutrient retention in microwave-heated food is complicated by a number of factors. Studies carried out prior to 1960 used ovens where wave frequency (usually 2450 Mhz), power input and output, voltage requirements and oven size were not consistently reported. Additionally, cooking parameters, such as the final internal temperature of the food, mass, load size, length of cooking and the product: water ratio (before and after cooking), were not well controlled. An added difficulty is that most studies focused on small quantities of food, comparable to domestic but not commercial applications. Reliable comparisons of nutrient retention in foods cooked by different methods were, therefore, not always possible. Reviews of the available data (Cross and Fung, 1982; Klein, 1982) suggests that microwave cooked food is, in general, likely to be comparable in nutrient composition to the equivalent food cooked conventionally.

Most of the studies in this area were carried out some time ago and need to be reassessed in light of changes in cooking and preparation procedures. More research is required using standardised procedures and cooking parameters to ascertain the effect of microwave heating on food, especially as this method has applications for large-scale catering.

Extrusion cooking

There are a number of other physical processing operations carried out by the food industry. One of the newest is extrusion cooking which is widely used in the production of pre-cooked starches (used in the manufacture of breakfast cereals, snack foods, confectionery fillers) and texturised vegetable proteins.

It is a continuous process using both temperature and pressure to expand mixtures which, on cooking, give products with a characteristic texture. Generally, a cereal flour or a protein mixture that has been moistened with steam or water is fed into an extruder barrel containing a screw. Heat is generated by friction and the barrel may additionally be heated by steam. Temperatures may approach 177°C and the pressure 500 psi at the die head which is fitted at the end of the barrel.

Under these conditions, the dough is flexible and will adapt to the die configuration. Upon leaving the die, the dough expands as the pressure is released. Moisture is flashed off and this cools the mixture. The final product usually contains 8–15% moisture and subsequent drying is often required.

Other common food processing operations include separation, mixing, milling, grinding, dispersion, emulsification, foaming and extrusion. The various manipulations used to modify foods give textures that make them acceptable. Such processes, unless they also involve heat, do not materially affect the nutritional quality of foods, except by making them more digestible and certainly much more attractive to eat.

CONCLUSIONS

The large number of variables that operate before, during and after processing make it almost impossible to predict precisely the effects of a particular processing operation on the nutrient content of the resulting food product. However, some general conclusions can be drawn.

In commercial processes such as chilling and freezing, the differences in nutrient content between the processed food, as cooked and ready to eat, and the same food cooked from the raw state (without processing) are relatively minor. In processes such as drying or evaporation where the resultant product is obviously different from the raw one, then losses of some of the more sensitive nutrients may occur. The degree to which these losses are considered important must be based on an appreciation of an individual's diet and the contribution the product makes to the nutrient content of the diet as a whole. It is the responsibility of the food industry to minimise these losses by carefully planned and controlled processing. It is the duty of government to monitor the diet of all sections of the population and undertake regular checks on the nutrient content of the more important foods available to the public. There can be no doubt that food processing in its broadest sense increases the consumers' accessibility to a varied range of foods throughout the year and so greatly facilitates the achievement of an adequate diet.

Acknowledgements

The Foundation wishes to record its thanks to Professor Alan Ward for his help in the drafting of this paper and to Campden Food Preservation Research Association for contributing some of the data quoted.

References

British Nutrition Foundation (1985). *Nutrition in catering.* Briefing Paper, No.4 (The British Nutrition Foundation, London)

Cross, G. A. and Fung, D. Y. C. (1982). The effect of microwaves on nutrient value of foods. *CRC Crit. Rev. Food Sci. Nutr.,* 16, 355-81

Department of Health and Social Security (1986). *Report on the safety and wholesomeness of irradiated foods.* Advisory Committee on Irradiated and Novel Foods. (DHSS, London)

Fennema, O. R. (1982). Effects of processing on nutritive values of food freezing. In Rechcigl Jnr., M. (ed.) *Handbook of nutritive value of processed food,* vol. 1, pp.31-44 (CRC Press Inc., Florida, USA)

Fennema, O. R. (1975). Effects of freeze-preservation on nutrients. In Harris, R. S. and Karmas, E. (eds.) pp. 244-88 *Nutritional evaluation of food processing.* (AVI Publishing Co., Inc., Westport, Connecticut, USA)

Food Additives and Contaminants Committee (1976). *Report on the review of flavourings in food.* FAC Report 22. (HMSO, London)

Harris, R. S. and Karmas, E. (eds.) (1975). *Nutritional evaluation of food processing,* 2nd Edn. (AVI Publishing, Co., Inc., Westport, Connecticut, USA)

Harris, R. S. and von Loesecke, H. (eds.) (1960) *Nutritional evaluation of food processing.* (John Wiley and Sons, New York)

Hunt, C. (1984). Nutrient losses in cook-freeze and cook-chill catering. *Human Nutr. App. Nutr.,* 38A, 50-9

Joint FAO/IAEA/WHO Expert Committee on the Wholesomeness of Irradiated Food (JECFI) (1981). *Report of the working party on irradiated food. WHO Technical Report Series,* 659.

Klein, B. P. (1982). Effects of processing on nutritive value of food: microwave cooking. In Rechcigl Jnr, M. (ed.) *Handbook of nutritive value of processed food,* vol. 1, pp. 209-36 (CRC Press Inc., Florida, USA)

Lamby, F. C. Farrow, R. P. and Elkins, E. R. (1982). Effects of processing on nutrient content and nutritional value of food: canning. In Rechcigl Jnr, M. (ed.) *Handbook of nutritive value of processed food,* vol. 1, pp. 11-30 (CRC Press Inc., Florida, USA)

Ministry of Agriculture, Fisheries and Food (1986). *1985 Household food consumption and expenditure:* Annual report of the National Food Survey Committee. (HMSO, London)

Rolls, B. A. (1982). Effect of processing on nutritive value of food: milk and milk products. In Rechcigl Jr, M. (ed.) *Handbook of nutritive value of processed food,* vol. 1, pp. 383-99 (CRC Press Inc., Florida, USA)

Index